NO ONE
EVER HAS
SEX
ON
HOLIDAY

BOOKS BY TRACY BLOOM

No-one Ever Has Sex on a Tuesday
No-one Ever Has Sex in the Suburbs
No-one Ever Has Sex on Christmas Day
No-one Ever Has Sex at a Wedding

Dinner Party
The Last Laugh
Single Woman Seeks Revenge
I Will Marry George Clooney by Christmas
Strictly My Husband

NO-ONE EVER HAS SEX ON HOLIDAY

TRACY BLOOM

bookouture

Published by Bookouture in 2019

An imprint of StoryFire Ltd.

Carmelite House
50 Victoria Embankment
London EC4Y 0DZ

www.bookouture.com

ISBN: 978-1-83888-026-2
eBook ISBN: 978-1-83888-025-5

For the policeman in the cool shades and curly moustache on CromerBeach in 1976, who single-handedly saved our family holiday because he found my dad's car keys.

Forever remembered!

Chapter One

Katy pulled up outside her house just after nine o'clock at night. She'd had the classic last day at work before going on holiday. Full of feverish anxiety and a desperate desire to get everything crossed off the to-do list, despite the fact many of the items had been lingering there for weeks. Even now, her head was still swirling, trying to think of all the things that could go wrong at the advertising agency whilst she was away. She really wasn't happy that the entire advertising campaign for the roll-out of Began, a new vegan bacon that tasted meatier than bacon, was going live without her there. It was a disaster waiting to happen, she just knew it. But what choice did she have? They had to go on holiday, right? It's what you do as a family. It's the highlight of your year. The reason why you spend twelve months slaving your guts out to spend a whole week with your nearest and dearest, having the time of your lives.

Except Katy couldn't quite envisage how you had the time of your life whilst battling with a stroppy nearly six-year-old and a terrible nearly two-year-old.

She took a deep breath and looked up at the house. She'd done nothing to get ready for the holiday. Nothing at all. Fortunately her husband Ben was a teacher and therefore had already had three weeks' holiday to accumulate piles of clothes on the spare bed and buy all the necessary travel accoutrements to guarantee a fun holiday with children. She prayed that he had remembered that they absolutely must not travel without Calpol, Sudocrem, swim nappies and adult paracetamol. Without these survival items the week could go horribly wrong. Of course the paracetamol on this holiday would be to cure headaches created by sharing one room with two small children rather than to remedy the daily hangovers that had been acquired on their pre-children holidays.

Katy picked up her laptop bag from the seat next to her and wondered if she would be able to sneak it into her luggage, hiding it amongst the nappies perhaps? Then at least she might be able to get that presentation done for the new client pitch she had in three weeks. That would really help with the inevitable tidal wave of work when she got back from holiday. She doubted she'd get away with that though. Ben had been very firm with her when they had booked the holiday that she needed to relax and leave her work behind. No emails, no computer, no phone calls, no nothing. Just quality family time, he'd said.

Deluded, she'd thought.

She'd heard many a horror story from friends who had already ventured to sunnier climes with young children. Wait until he'd spent the fifth day in a row building sandcastles and then see if he would jump at the chance for a conversation on the phone about something other than how does one get all the sand out of a nappy bag?

Time to embrace it, she thought, getting out of the car. This was their first proper holiday abroad with two children. It was going to be great. Splashing in the pool, playing in the sand and enjoying fabulous Mediterranean food with maybe the odd glass of wine. Not to mention spending time with some of their closest friends. Ben's best mate 'Braindead' was going with his wife Abby and fifteen-month-old son Logan as well as Katy's close friend and colleague Daniel, who was bringing his husband Gabriel and their daughter Silvie, who was just nine months old. It was going to be a riot, right?

But it would probably not be like previous holidays with Ben before they had kids, which would have involved lying by the pool, swimming in the sea, goldfish-bowl cocktails and actually rather a lot of sex. That reminded her. They really should perhaps fit a quick one in tonight as there was certainly going be no action next week sharing a room with two kids. Perhaps she should point this out to Ben, as long as she wasn't too tired after packing.

She opened the front door and could hear what sounded like some kind of rave coming from the sitting room. There was very loud music playing and much shouting. She walked into the room to find Ben and Millie jumping up and down on the sofa, singing at the tops of their voices. Jack was crouching on the hearthrug, banging some bricks together.

'We're going on a trip, we're going on a trip, it won't be in a ship, it won't be in a ship,' they chanted.

'Hello Mummy,' boomed Ben as soon as he caught sight of her. He leapt off the sofa and went to turn down the music that was blaring out of the speaker.

'What are you doing?' she asked, wondering if she had the time wrong. Both Millie and Jack would normally have been in bed ages ago.

'I'm trying to keep them awake so that they sleep on the flight tomorrow,' he said.

There was certain logic there, thought Katy, however she suspected it could go either way. Yes, they could fall angelically asleep for the entire flight, making it a hugely enjoyable experience, or they could be massively overtired and cranky and make it the flight from hell. Since they were getting up at the crack of dawn anyway to get to the airport, she suspected the odds of a stress-free flight were not in their favour.

'Daddy says we are all going to build the biggest sandcastle ever,' chipped in Millie. 'Taller than me!'

'Wow, that's cool,' replied Katy, wondering how soon it would take toddler Jack to crush their dreams of sandcastle nirvana.

She stopped. She needed to give herself a good talking-to. This holiday was going to be fun. Of course it was. Look at the excited looks on Ben and Millie's faces and the excited dribble coming out of Jack's mouth.

'I can't wait,' said Katy, putting a forced grin on her face and picking Millie up in her arms and swirling her round. 'I really can't.'

*

It was midnight when Katy got to bed and she felt like crying.

Ben had done a tremendous job of laying all the clothes out on the spare bed but hadn't thought it necessary to iron them so they were all a crumpled mess. There was no way Katy was ironing on holiday so at ten o'clock, she'd got the ironing board out and set about ironing all the clothes and carefully putting them into suitcases. It's okay, she'd thought, tomorrow I get to sit by a pool and do nothing all day. I can sleep then. Possibly. If the kids sleep too.

Ben had also forgotten to buy kids' sun cream, which wasn't his fault as it wasn't on the list. Katy knew they could probably get it at the chemist in the airport but Millie had had an allergic reaction to a sun cream last year so they had to use a particular one and, if they didn't have it, it would be a disaster. So Ben spent half an hour trying to locate a late-opening pharmacy that stocked the sun cream they needed then drove off into the night, saying he would come back with a takeaway because in a fit of over-organisation he'd already cleared the fridge of food.

He arrived back just after 11 p.m. as Katy was clearing away the ironing board and they sat watching the telly in exhausted silence, munching on Chinese food.

As Katy bit into a spare rib she remembered that she hadn't sent an email to their finance director about a budget cut to one of the campaigns. She grabbed her phone and fired the email off, knowing that if she didn't do it now, she might forget.

'You will try and switch off from work this holiday, won't you?' Ben asked her as she furiously typed into her phone with one hand whilst dangling the rib in the other.

She nodded, her mouth full and her concentration focused elsewhere.

'I had a text from Braindead earlier,' he said when she'd put her phone down. 'Asking if they'd be okay to take four cases onto the plane.'

'Good God,' spluttered Katy. 'What are they taking with them? Logan's cot or something? They've only got one child coming with them, why on earth do they need four cases?'

'I said that,' replied Ben. 'Braindead said Abby needs a case just for her going-out clothes.'

'Going-out clothes? She does realise what kind of holiday this is, doesn't she? I mean, she has a baby now. There won't be much going out on the town happening, will there? We'll be lucky to enjoy a drink in the hotel bar.'

'Braindead's so excited about coming with us, you know,' said Ben. 'It's been ages since me and him have been on holiday together.'

'Where did you last go with him?'

'Faliraki was our last big boys' trip. Braindead got arrested.'

'What for?'

'Impersonating a police officer… whilst dancing naked on a podium in a club.'

'Wow,' said Katy. 'How do you impersonate a police officer whilst naked?'

'I can't remember,' replied Ben. 'But Braindead, being Braindead, managed it.'

Katy felt a slight fluttering in her chest at the thought of the implications of taking Ben's best friend on holiday with them. It wasn't that Braindead was stupid, far from it. He was one of the smartest people that Katy had ever met; he just had a very strange way of showing it. He saw things in a very different way to the rest of the universe. Hence his nickname, which Ben had given him at school and which everyone now used rather than his real name, which was a very sensible-sounding Craig. To be honest though, he'd mellowed since the birth of his son Logan just over a year ago. He was now the epitome of a doting dad and was totally and utterly smitten. So maybe this newer, more mature Braindead was safe to go on holiday with.

'I guess he is a father now,' Katy said. 'Not sure he'll be doing any naked podium dancing this holiday,' she added. 'We're more likely to see that sort of behaviour from Logan. Is he still taking his clothes off at any opportunity?'

'Seems so,' replied Ben. 'Apparently Braindead lost him in the fruit and veg section of the supermarket the other day. Found him fondling potatoes with his clothes in a pile next to him. Braindead reckons he's going to be a naturist. He'll have a beard and wrinkly bottom by the time he's three.'

Katy thought briefly about the chaos that Logan, the fifteen-month-old stripper, and Jack, the nearly two-year-old toddler, could bring to the holiday and shuddered slightly. At least having kids around would mean that no-one was likely to get arrested, she figured. That would be a bonus.

'Did you see Daniel today?' Ben asked. 'Did they get Silvie's passport okay?'

'Well yes, just in time. Can't believe they forgot they'd need one for her. I think he was a bit disappointed with the passport office though.'

'Why? Did they make a fuss? I did wonder if it would be difficult, what with her being a surrogate baby and having two dads and that.'

'No actually. They made no fuss at all. It was all dead easy, Daniel said. I think he was expecting the red carpet treatment, you know. I think he wanted to feel special and unique, like there should be a separate channel for surrogate babies and gay dads or something. You know what he's like. He's all for being treated like an equal but what he really wants is to be seen as some unique pioneer and he gets upset when he's treated like he's just normal.'

'That's why I still can't believe he wanted to come on holiday with us,' Ben observed. 'A package-style holiday in Spain? I can't see him fitting in at all, can you? He has such a poor attitude when it comes to mixing with the masses. He won't even watch *Pointless* on TV for fear he might be contaminated.'

'Oh, I have no doubt that Daniel didn't want to come really but Gabriel was keen. Gabriel wants to make sure that Silvie has as normal an upbringing as possible. Apparently Daniel suggested a safari in Kenya but Gabriel put his foot down.'

'But Gabriel is Spanish! Surely he would want to do authentic Spain, not Brits-abroad Spain?' said Ben.

'Perhaps he thinks it's the perfect way for Silvie to experience both cultures at the same time?' replied Katy.

'So we should put him in a sombrero, take him down to the Irish bar and buy him a pint of Guinness and then have a good old sing-song on the karaoke,' said Ben nodding thoughtfully.

'Heaven knows what he's going to think,' replied Katy, shaking her head. 'He may never see his beloved home country in the same way again!'

*

Katy set her alarm for five in the morning so they could be ready for the taxi to pick them up at six. She was already worrying about whether that was long enough to get two small excitable children dressed and fed and ready to get out of the door.

'You know we're sharing a room with the kids on holiday,' Ben whispered in her ear just as she closed her eyes.

'I know,' she said. 'But I'm knackered. Sorry. Can we just go to sleep? Maybe we'll get the chance to leave the kids with everyone else one night and sneak off.'

'Good idea,' Ben whispered. 'I'm sure that will happen. Night, night. Happy holidays.'

Chapter Two

'What do you think of this one?' asked Abby. 'Braindead? Look at this one. It's blue, you see, goes with those green shoes I bought last week in the sale. Remember I told you. Braindead, are you listening?'

'What?' said Braindead, jerking his head up. He was lying on the floor, pushing a train up and down in front of Logan, making the puffing noises and everything. He was very proud of his puffing noises. He'd spent some time perfecting them and now he was pretty much a pitch-perfect copy of Spencer out of *Thomas the Tank Engine*.

'What do you think of this dress?' asked Abby again. 'I bought it today. To take on holiday.'

Braindead looked at it. It was blue.

'You look great,' he said, grinning at Logan and pretending to drive the train over his leg, making more desperate puffing noises. Logan chuckled in delight. Braindead gathered up another train and drove that one over his head, making a whining sound as it reached the summit.

'Daddy,' laughed Logan, clapping his hands.

'He said Daddy again,' Braindead said, looking up at Abby.

'I know, you tell me every time,' she replied before disappearing out the room.

'This was a bargain,' she said reappearing, this time in silver sequins. 'I reckon it's leftover stock from Christmas but you could so wear it on holiday. Because it's strapless. And it goes with those diamante shoes I bought last week.'

Braindead glanced up. His wife looked like she was ready to go down to Valentine's nightclub in Leeds, not packing for a family holiday in Spain.

He had no idea why she needed so much stuff. As far as he was concerned all they needed were a couple of T-shirts, some shorts and swimming stuff. No more than that. Although he had bought Logan some really cool Spider-Man swimming shorts online. He couldn't resist. Oh, and a shark-fin swimming hat and a massive doughnut-shaped float that he would be able to push him round the pool in. Logan couldn't be seen without the proper kit. That was a given.

'Should I take it, do you think?' Abby asked him as she twirled round in the dress. 'I do have another silver dress already packed.'

'Why?' he asked her. 'It's not like we'll be going out to clubs or anything, is it? Not with this little chap in tow. Kids' club maybe but I think you would be a bit overdressed for the sandpit in that.'

Abby stopped twirling and stared at Braindead. Her shoulders sagged.

'You never wear ninety per cent of the clothes you take on holiday anyway,' he continued. 'It's like a rule. You should pack and then halve it. Especially for this little streaker,' he said, tickling his son. 'He's unlikely to wear anything at all. Going to come back brown as a berry, aren't you, chap? That reminds me, have we got sunblock for Logan's winky? We need to look after that little fella.'

'I've not packed anything for Logan,' replied Abby. 'I thought you were doing that?'

'Oh right,' said Braindead. 'Yeah, sure. No problem. Come on, chap,' he said, swinging Logan up into his arms. 'You, me and a suitcase have got some serious clothes wrangling to do. And don't you worry. Winky sunblock will be purchased… somewhere. I'll call Ben. Perhaps he's got some.'

*

'There's some really cool bars near where we are staying,' said Abby as they sat down to eat once the four suitcases plus nappy bag were lined up in the hall ready for their early morning pick-up. 'Cheryl at work said there are some amazing cocktail bars in the town. She said she'd had the best negroni she had ever tasted there.'

'Negroni?' asked Braindead. 'What's that?'

'A cocktail!'

'A cocktail that has groan in the middle of it? Is that the groan for the hangover it's going to give you?'

'I wouldn't know,' replied Abby sharply. 'I've never had one.'

'It's going to be good, isn't it, going on holiday with everyone?' said Braindead. 'Be great for Jack and Logan to spend the week together. How cool is that? Their first lads' holiday and still in nappies!'

'They won't remember it.'

'But we will,' replied Braindead. 'Our first family holiday. You don't forget that, do you? And we get to share it with Ben and Katy.'

'That is a bonus,' said Abby. 'I'm already eyeing them up to babysit whilst we have a couple of nights out, drinking negronis.'

'Oh,' said Braindead. 'Not sure how that will work. I mean, where would we put Logan to bed?'

'He could bed down with Ben and Katy.'

'But Logan doesn't sleep through the night. He'll wake them up and Millie and Jack.'

Abby stared back at him. 'I'm very aware he doesn't sleep through the night,' she replied. 'These bags under my eyes are painfully aware that we haven't had a full night's sleep in forever.' She bit her lip. 'Which is why I need to go and get absolutely smashed on negronis on holiday to try and forget that fact and I shall be doing that with or without you.'

He watched as she got up. They never argued before Logan arrived. Neither of them had taken life seriously enough. Turned out that sheer exhaustion somehow made life a lot more serious.

*

An hour later, Braindead climbed into bed beside Abby. He curled up behind her and wrapped his arm over the side of her body. She smelled amazing. She always smelled amazing. Like she showered in water entirely different to him. He didn't understand why Abby wanted to go out partying whilst they were on holiday. He'd been there, done that and literally bought the T-shirt. From Faliraki, if he remembered correctly. *I survived the Faliraki Pizza Challenge* was still a favourite that he often wore for bed. It reminded him of that infamous night when he ate an entire twenty-four-inch pizza. Possibly one of the most triumphant nights of his life. But he wouldn't want to go back to that sort of holiday. No way. He couldn't wait to take Logan to the beach for the first time and build sandcastles with him and paddle in the sea. In fact, Braindead thought he had never been more excited about going on holiday than this one. His first as a dad. Their first as a family.

He cuddled up behind Abby and she snuggled back, pushing up against him. That was normally the sign that sex could be welcome but he wasn't sure after her earlier outburst. But opportunities had been very few and far between recently since the arrival of Logan. Maybe he should go for it. Who knew when they might get another chance? He reached his arm around, putting his hand under her camisole top. She moaned quietly. They were on. A small cry emerged from the baby monitor beside his bed. He froze. All was quiet. He gently stroked Abby's belly. She didn't push his hand away. Another cry came through the monitor, then another and then a full-on wail. He got out of bed and went through to Logan's room.

Chapter Three

'Hi honeys, I'm home,' shouted Daniel as he pushed open the door of their apartment in the fashionable waterfront area of Leeds. He placed his workbag on the occasional table in the hall and walked through into the vast open space of the kitchen-cum-living-room, cum-dining-room, cum-newly-allocated-play-area. And there they were. Gabriel, his husband of almost two years, with Silvie, their nine-month-old little baby girl, nestling on his chest. They looked like they both should be in some arty black and white photo shoot, the scene was so gorgeous. Daniel gasped slightly and just watched for a moment before walking into the room.

'I bought you both something,' he declared, dangling a large Harvey Nichols carrier bag in front of him.

'Oh Daniel,' said Gabriel in his still fairly thick Spanish accent. 'You must stop spoiling us.'

'Nonsense,' said Daniel. 'That's my job.' The truth was that Daniel really did think it was his job. It had been decided from the moment they said they wanted children that Gabriel would be the one to stay at home and care for the baby and Daniel would carry on working, which secretly he had been mightily relieved about. He'd offered of course. Offered to give up his well-paid position as creative director at the Butler & Calder Advertising Agency and stay at home all day, every day, changing nappies and watching daytime TV, but only after

Gabriel had said that if they were lucky enough to get a child then he would really like the privilege of staying home and being a full-time parent. Daniel had never been more relieved but his guilt was driving him into overkill on the role of 'provider' of the family. He found he was constantly looking for stuff to buy to make Gabriel's and Silvie's life at home as marvellous as possible.

'Look,' he said, pulling his latest purchase out of the thick cardboard bag. 'It's a faux leather baby-changing rucksack. You can wear it across your body or on your back. It has a detachable clutch, handy for nappy changes. It comes with an insulated bottle holder as well as a padded changing mat. Oh, and it has a sleeve for your laptop so that you can browse the net whilst you're in a café having a flat white. And of course it's wipe-clean and water-resistant. I checked. Isn't it fabulous?'

'But we already have a changing bag?' said Gabriel.

'I know, but I, well, I thought this might be better for our holiday. It matches our suitcases and everything.'

'You mean you were worried that the cartoon cowboy plastic one didn't match?' asked Gabriel.

'I know you love it,' said Daniel, 'but I can't deny that it upsets me. Just a bit. To even look at it.'

Gabriel laughed. 'Well, it's a good bag,' he nodded. 'Thank you. I'm sure you will enjoy showing it off in Spain surrounded by many families who appear to be coping quite well with their plastic, primary-coloured nappy bags.'

'Oh God,' replied Daniel. 'You're right. It'll be nappy bag central. It will be some kind of hell!'

'It's all right,' replied Gabriel, still laughing. 'You can go and sit at the bar with the other dads and drink beer whilst I share notes on what's best for nappy rash with the mums.'

Daniel put his head in his hands. It had seemed like such a good idea to plan a holiday with people who had children. Friends to help out as they tried to navigate their way through becoming the parents of a little baby girl. And, after all, they were going to go with Katy who had two children so she must know what she was doing? She had to be a pair of safe hands.

Turned out he needn't have worried. Gabriel was the most natural dad you could ever imagine. He'd grown up with a whole tribe of younger siblings and had the instant ability to incorporate children into everyday life, which seemed so much the Spanish way. To some extent Daniel felt like a bit of a spare part and, unusually for him, a complete novice. He liked to be the expert on most things and hated having to ask Gabriel constantly for help and advice on even the basics such as changing nappies and cleaning bottles. Daniel was actually pretty useless when it came to babies and so Gabriel tended to do everything as he did it better and quicker. This left Daniel feeling what he thought it must feel like to be in a heterosexual relationship. Something he'd never expected to experience and something he had taken great steps to avoid. He was the husband to a very domesticated and highly proficient parent who made him feel inadequate in the home and, if he was honest, slightly resentful. He tried not to show this reaction, of course, as he was very aware of how lucky he was that Gabriel was so willing to take care of the home front, but it left a slightly uncomfortable taste in his mouth that they had somehow slipped into such traditional male/female roles in their marriage.

'I shall not be sitting by the bar with the other dads,' declared Daniel. 'Sit and listen to them talk football and what other people's wives look like in bikinis? I don't think so. I'd prefer to sit at the bar with you, with Silvie on my lap whilst we sip on a cocktail or two. That is how I wish to get through this holiday.'

Daniel took Silvie from Gabriel and balanced her over his shoulder. He began to bounce up and down and immediately a whimper came out of Silvie's mouth. He felt himself tense and then the wail came. A full-on, wide-open-mouth, piercing wail.

'There, there,' he said, patting her back. 'There, there, far, far, near, near, so, so.'

Silvie continued to wail. Daniel daren't look at Gabriel. He couldn't bear to see the sympathetic amazement that Daniel had an instant ability to wind up their baby.

Daniel bounced ever harder and inexplicably began singing 'Rock Around the Clock'. He was baffled by a baby's ability to lead you down such ridiculous paths but somehow it happened.

The sounds of the fifties were clearly doing nothing to calm poor Silvie and so eventually Daniel decided he'd switch to something more recent and began singing 'Sex on Fire' by Kings of Leon, much to his astonishment. This wouldn't do by the pool in Spain – he was going to have to have some songs in his armoury with less innuendo for soothing Silvie.

Silvie was getting no better and eventually he felt Gabriel gently extract her from his shoulder and nestle her in the crook of his arm where, as if by magic, she instantly calmed down and gurgled contentedly.

Daniel stared down at the happy baby and sighed. He hadn't expected fatherhood to feel this way. He hadn't expected his skills to be judged so emphatically poorly. That hadn't happened to him in a long while. He'd got himself to a stage in life where he was good at what he did and used to being endlessly praised and even given awards for how proficient he was. And here this little mite thought he couldn't do shit. How did you deal with that?

Gabriel looked at him so sympathetically, which made it a whole lot worse. What must he think when Daniel couldn't even hold their own daughter without her bursting into tears?

'I'll go and get the suitcases down,' said Daniel, gathering himself. 'Start packing. I need to decide exactly how many outfits one needs for a holiday of a package nature. Something I have never had to contemplate before.'

'Oh, we already packed this morning,' said Gabriel, wiping some drool from Silvie's chin with a muslin cloth. 'I hope you don't mind but I laid some clothes out on the bed for you. I've picked some stuff out that I thought you might need. Oh, and we went to the chemist and bought all the essentials.'

'What, like sun protection and insect repellent?'

'No, I mean for Silvie. Nappy cream and wipes and swim nappies.'

'Right,' said Daniel. 'Of course. I'll go and finish off then.'

*

He gazed down at the clothes lying on the bed, waiting for his brain to make his selection of what to pack. Gabriel had of course got it spot on. Linen shorts and trousers, some very expensive designer T-shirts and multiple going-out shirts in varying shades of the rainbow. His holiday wardrobe had been excellently curated by his husband, leaving him only the job of lifting the carefully folded items off the bed and into the suitcase. Job done. He was all ready to go.

He was such a lucky man to have such a proficient husband. And it was going to be a great holiday, spending time with friends and their children. He must try and ignore the nagging concerns about the budget airline flight being packed with drunken hen and stag parties and the hotel being overrun with rugrats, swarming round all the time.

No, it wasn't going to be like that at all. It was going to be absolutely blissful.

Chapter Four

Katy knew they would be the first to arrive at the airport but she hadn't expected Daniel to be the last. And certainly not to start the holiday looking so flustered.

'We overslept,' he said, dashing up to them, car seat in one hand and pushchair in the other. 'We forgot to set the alarm. The taxi driver leaning on the doorbell woke us up.'

'Well, you're here now,' sighed Katy. 'But we've already lost Braindead and Abby.'

Braindead had arrived and instantly said he needed food so had ambled off to join the café queue with Logan in tow whilst Abby said she needed something from the newsagent and had left Katy and Ben with Millie straining on Ben's hand and Jack banging his feet against the pushchair. Next to them were two trolleys piled high with suitcases and car seats and all sorts of kid paraphernalia. Katy and Ben looked like they had just been made homeless and were out on the streets with all their worldly goods.

Gabriel walked up with baby Silvie strapped to his front, looking neat and tidy and calm, pushing his trolley carefully stacked with matching suitcases.

'Bloody hell,' muttered Ben. 'Do you think we have enough kit? Do you think they're even going to let us on the plane?'

'I am panicking,' admitted Katy. 'It is a budget airline, after all. They'll let us on the plane but they could charge us the cost of several more seats to get all this baggage on.'

'I told you not to book a budget airline,' said Daniel. 'False economy every time.'

'But it would have been double on any other airline. I thought we could spend what we save on a better hotel. After all, that is going to be where we spend most of our time. It's only a two-and-a-half-hour flight.'

Daniel gave Katy a knowing look. Like she was a stupid, disillusioned fool. It was the first time she'd been on holiday with Daniel. They were the best of friends and she loved working with him but this could be a whole new ball game. They'd been on the odd business trip together, short hops over to mainland Europe, but that had typically been in business class, where there was a degree of comfort and pampering. She feared travelling with Daniel with four children in tow on an airline that treated its customers like cattle was going to be a challenging experience. Daniel was not one to stay quiet if he felt like service was poor.

Thankfully, Braindead reappeared just then, eating a cheese and onion pasty and carrying a large cardboard cup of tea.

'Abby with you?' asked Katy.

'No, I thought she'd be here.'

'She went to the newsagents.'

'Shall I go and get her?'

'No!' said Katy and Ben in unison, knowing that could be the last they saw of both of them for some time.

'I'll go get her,' said Katy. 'You stay here.' She felt stressed. She feared herding cats could become the theme of the entire trip.

'It's all right, she's here,' said Braindead, nodding down the corridor.

They all turned to be greeted by the sight of Abby tottering down the corridor in full make-up, short skirt, low-cut top and sky-high shoes. Perfect travel wear for going on a plane with small children.

'Bloody hell, Abby, you going on a hen party or a family holiday?' said Daniel.

Exactly what I was thinking, thought Katy, glancing down at her cut-off jeans, cotton top and trainers, knowing it was likely she would be spending most of the flight walking up and down the aisle with Jack tottering between her legs. Katy had never felt more over forty as she surveyed Abby's twenty-five-year-old slim build exposed by skimpy clothing, despite the fact she was also a mother. Katy privately congratulated herself on not packing a bikini. She couldn't compete with Abby.

'Right,' announced Katy. 'Are we all here now? Have you all got your passports and tickets?'

'Yes, Mum,' mumbled everyone whilst patting pockets or feeling inside bags. Katy already hated the fact that inevitably she was going to have to be the one in charge on this trip. She'd booked it and so she was going to be the one that they all looked to to keep them organised. It was *exactly* like being at work.

*

'This is a very long queue,' stated Daniel as they came to a stop at the end of the check-in line.

Katy thought she was already ready to kill someone.

'Is there not a fast-track queue or something we can pay to join?' he asked. 'I mean, this could take at least half an hour. To check in? That's just outrageous with small children. Do they not have a family queue? Surely if you're travelling with small children they know that you need preferential treatment. You can't make babies wait half an hour to check in for a flight, can you?'

'This flight cost us less than getting a train from Leeds to London. There will be no preferential treatment for anyone, believe me,' stated Katy. 'Look, Daniel. Think of this as like a consumer research project. You will be experiencing how most normal people travel, those without expense accounts and high-paying careers. Queuing to check in is normal. Sitting in business class sipping champagne is not.'

'I can do normal,' protested Daniel. 'I do normal all the time.'

'What was the last normal thing you did?' she asked him. 'Where you didn't expect to get treated as special?'

Daniel stared back at her.

He looked around awkwardly.

'I er… I er… rang and booked my own table at Quados last week.'

'You managed to pick up the phone and book a table at a Michelin-starred restaurant? Congratulations, Daniel, you are truly normal,' said Katy sarcastically.

'I can do normal!' protested Daniel. 'You just wait and see. I will be the normal-looking one on this budget airline flight. I will take it in my stride, I will blend into the background as though I am totally used to chronically bad service and being squashed against way too many synthetic fibres. I am going to blend in as though I am one of the masses, just you wait and see. Oh my God!' he said, his eyes flaring wide as he looked over Katy's shoulders. 'What have you made me do?'

Katy turned round to see a man with a beard, dressed in a Babygro with a dummy round his neck, join the queue behind them. He was followed by several more adult males in a variety of colours of Babygro, as well as a man in just a large nappy, a vest and pink booties. He was clearly the unfortunate groom on his way to a lively-looking stag party.

Katy glanced over at Daniel, who was staring at the group. He looked pale as he leaned over towards Gabriel and whispered in his ear.

'Did you pack the Valium?' he asked him.

*

When they eventually got to the check-in desk there was an altercation over the number of car seats they were travelling with and at one point Katy thought she was going to have to restrain Daniel, who didn't know how to deal with the airline representative's insolent tone.

'Daniel!' she said. 'Go and stand over there. You are *not* helping.'

'But she's being a prick,' said Daniel.

'I will be calling my supervisor,' said the woman, 'if you don't get this man out of my face.'

'I am not in your face,' replied Daniel. 'I do not want to be anywhere near your stupid—'

'Daniel!' shouted Katy. 'Over there before we are all banned from flying.'

'Come on, mate,' said Ben, taking his arm and leading him to one side. 'It really doesn't help getting angry, believe me.'

'But I don't understand. Where is their level of customer service?' protested Daniel, looking confused.

'They don't have any. Just deal with it. That's why it's so cheap.'

'So we'll pay to put one of the car seats in the hold,' offered Katy, turning back to the woman. 'If that's what it takes to get us on this flight.'

'It's normally the stag dos that give us grief at the desk,' the woman said to her. 'Not the families. Have a nice flight,' she added with a grimace, handing back the passports.

*

'Hang on,' said Gabriel as they cleared security. 'Brainy hasn't got through yet.'

'Can you please call him Braindead?' asked Ben. 'It's so confusing when you call him Brainy.'

Gabriel smiled at Ben and put his hand on his shoulder. 'But I think that Brainy suits him so much more, don't you?'

Ben looked back towards the scanning machines where Braindead, Abby and Logan were still occupied. Abby and Logan had come through but Braindead appeared to be in an altercation with the pushchair and was currently engaged in trying to ram it into the hole to get it through the scanner.

This could end really badly, thought Ben.

Suddenly an alarm went off and an orange light started flashing on top of the scanner. Uniforms moved swiftly and surrounded Braindead, pulling him away from the machine and the offending buggy. A male security guard gripped his arm tightly as two others grabbed hold of the buggy and started yanking it with some force.

'The Bugaboo,' shrieked Abby. 'That cost more than this holiday.'

Ben watched frozen to the spot, unsure what to do. He daren't go and help, as he feared that making a dash through the people scanner would look mighty suspicious.

A further uniformed man approached and joined the other two in their battle with the buggy and the security scanner, which both seemed unwilling to let each other go. By this time the people in the queue behind Braindead were tutting and showing signs of revolt as they looked at their watches and tapped their feet impatiently.

'We'll need an engineer,' someone finally declared. 'It's jammed. Can you get Mike on the radio?'

'Tell Mike I'm sorry,' said Braindead, looking very sorry for himself. 'I didn't mean to break anything. Can I still go on holiday?'

None of the assembled uniforms replied.

'I can't watch,' announced Katy, standing behind Ben and Gabriel. 'I think I might join the stag do in the bar. I think their trip might be less chaotic than ours.'

'Why don't you all go for a coffee and I'll wait here for Braindead,' said Ben. 'Who knows how this is going to pan out. I didn't read anything in the FAQs about what to do if you manage to break security!'

*

'Why are we standing here?' asked Daniel an hour later after Braindead had finally been allowed through after the Bugaboo had been completely dismantled. It was now in bits in a large duty-free bag. 'It's still thirty minutes until we board.'

'Because if we don't stand and wait at the front of the line we may not be able to sit together,' replied Ben.

'What do you mean, we might not be able to sit together? Aren't our seats allocated?' asked Daniel.

'No,' replied Ben. 'It's first come, first served.'

Daniel turned to look at him with a look of utter horror.

'What? Like a bus?'

'Yes,' replied Ben. 'I can't believe you have never been on a budget airline before. Surely you knew that?'

Daniel gazed around him in shock. 'So we have to be at the front of the queue?'

'Yep,' nodded Ben.

'And just wait?'

'Yep.'

'This is already the worst holiday I have ever been on.'

'Welcome to the real world, Daniel.'

*

'Oi,' shouted Daniel as an elderly couple overtook him along the gangway leading onto the plane. 'Oi! We were in front of you in the queue. We're getting on this plane first. Don't you know the seats are not allocated? You can't push in like that!'

The elderly couple did not look back. They were either deaf or pretending to be deaf. They were sitting on the front row by the time Daniel had battled through the door of the plane with car seats and the new changing rucksack and fumbled with the tickets out of his pocket. The elderly couple looked up at Daniel innocently as he went to walk past them.

He tapped Katy on the shoulder, and she turned around looking totally and utterly harassed. Jack was smearing chocolate over her flushed face and she was struggling to keep the over-packed nappy bag under control as she made her way up the narrow aisle.

Daniel shook his head in disbelief.

'I have absolutely no idea how to enjoy this holiday,' he announced desperately.

Katy blinked back at him as Jack stuffed his hand in her mouth.

'Neither have I,' she mumbled back.

Chapter Five

'Just grab a seat,' shouted Katy as they approached some clear rows. 'We can reorganise ourselves after we take off. Just grab a seat!' She had to calm down. It was like the first day of the sales. This wasn't the relaxing start to the holiday that she had hoped for.

They piled into three rows of seats, nappy bags, car seats and the bag of broken Bugaboo being flung here, there and everywhere in order to claim their spot. Gabriel and Braindead ended up in a row of three with Silvie on Gabriel's knee and Logan plonked firmly between them. Then Ben managed to commandeer an entire row for him, Millie and Jack, leaving Abby, Katy and Daniel to fill up the row behind them. That would do for now, thought Katy, sitting down between Daniel and Abby.

'I am clenching my buttocks so tight,' announced Daniel once he'd fastened his seatbelt and arranged his magazine and newspaper in the pocket in front of him.

'What's up now?' she asked.

'What happens if the Baby Stag Party ends up sitting near to us? Are there face masks provided because I don't think I can look at grown men in Babygros, drinking the bar dry.'

'Looks like the steward is sending them to the back of the plane out of everyone's way,' said Katy as the overgrown babies trooped past them, already swaying, no doubt with one too many pints inside them.

'Don't make eye contact,' hissed Daniel. 'Everyone look at the floor and hopefully they'll just walk straight past.'

They both went quiet, pretending to study the safety instructions.

'Is this seat taken?' a voice piped up.

They looked up and there was a lady in her mid-forties pointing at the seat opposite the aisle to Daniel. She looked harmless enough and she certainly wasn't dressed in babywear. She was large; her body rippled under her pink striped T-shirt and three-quarter-length trousers.

'Oh no, please,' said Daniel. 'You take this seat. Can I help you with anything?'

'Oi,' shouted the lady down the aisle. 'There's enough room here for us all. Get a shift on. If you wouldn't mind holding my duty-free,' she said, handing a large bag over to Daniel as a gaggle of twenty-something girls in pink sparkly cowboy hats and matching T-shirts oozed into the remaining seats surrounding the group.

Daniel exchanged a glance with Katy. He shook his head slowly.

'That's better,' said the woman, kicking off her shoes and taking the bag back from Daniel. She delved inside and pulled out a stack of paper cups and a bottle of vodka.

'Right, ladies,' she said, pulling down the lap tray and splashing the liquid into the cups. 'Get some of this down you before old frosty knickers at the front comes and confiscates it.'

Paper cups were passed along rows and over heads and across the aisle until everyone had one.

'Here, have one,' the woman said to Daniel when she caught him staring at her. 'Just don't grass us up to the trolley dollies.'

Daniel glanced back at Katy and then shrugged in a 'if you can't beat 'em join 'em' kind of way. He stuck his hand out. 'Why not?' he said. 'I could do with it.'

'My name's Ruth,' the woman told him. 'We're on a hen do. You on a family holiday, I take it,' she said, nodding at Katy and Abby.

Daniel gasped in shock. 'This is not my wife and I am certainly not old enough to have a daughter of Abby's age or dress sense. No, my husband and baby daughter are in the row in front there, look.'

'I see,' nodded Ruth. 'Aren't you just the adorable things? Would your husband care to join us?'

'Not for me, but *gracias*, that is very kind,' Gabriel replied, turning round, clearly having been listening to every word.

'He's foreign?' said Ruth to Daniel. 'Good-looking and holding the baby. You punched above your weight, didn't you?'

Daniel gasped in shock whilst Katy threw back her head and laughed.

'You are so right,' said Katy, leaning forward to address Ruth. 'I've no idea how he managed it either.'

'Oi you,' said Daniel. 'I'll have you know I'm a catch.'

'Clearly hidden qualities,' said Ruth, raising her eyebrows at Katy. 'Vodka?'

Katy glanced at Daniel who had already knocked back his drink and was now actually looking a lot more relaxed.

'Why not,' she nodded. 'It seems to have cheered up the miseries amongst us. Today has to get better somehow.'

Ruth handed her over yet another cup from the seemingly never-ending supply in her bag. 'And your friend next to you?' she asked, indicating Abby.

'Oh yes please,' said Abby, eagerly leaning forward. 'Thought you'd never ask.'

'Where are you staying?' asked Katy once more alcohol had been distributed.

'The Consuella,' answered Ruth.

'Oh,' said Katy. 'I think that's just down the road from us. We're at the Romano.'

'Well, I'm sure yours is much fancier than ours. Ours is a dump but it's only for a few nights. We'll spend our money on giving Cassie a proper good time.'

'So who's the lucky lady?' asked Abby.

'Cassie,' said Ruth, turning to address the person next to her. 'Stand up, chick, and say hello to my new friends.'

A young girl stood up and rather timidly gave them a wave. They waved back.

'Is she your daughter?' asked Daniel.

'You cheeky bastard,' admonished Ruth.

'Touché, I think,' replied Daniel with a sly grin.

'We're colleagues actually,' said Ruth. 'Cassie works in my team but we're like one big happy family at Spendloves. I always organise the hen parties. The girls love it. They come to me and say they are getting married and I say, right, you tell me where, when, guest list, budget and I'll sort it. One year I did do three actually, which I nearly had a breakdown over, but never mind, it was worth it.'

'So you're like a professional hen party organiser but you do it just for your mates and your colleagues?' asked Abby in awe. 'And you always go along. How cool is that?'

'That's right. I've got it down to a fine art by now of course. Which reminds me,' she said, looking at her watch. 'It's time. Hold that, will you?' She handed the vodka bottle over to Daniel. 'Be careful not to let the stewards see it or they'll take it off you. Help yourself.'

Ruth leant down between her legs and fished a parcel out of her carry-on bag. Daniel poured a generous amount of vodka into his cup before topping up Katy and Abby.

'Pass the parcel time, girls,' said Ruth, standing up and turning to face the seats behind her. 'Pass this round and every time I shout "Cock and Bull", if you're holding the parcel you have to peel a layer off and do whatever it says in the piece of paper inside. Sneak the vodka round first,' she added in a stage whisper, taking the bottle from Daniel and passing it to the girls in the row behind him.

'You joining us?' Ruth asked Daniel. 'I think snog a gay man *is* on one of the challenges so if you join in and you get that one, you are quids in, hey? Although saying that, I think I want that one and then I can have a go at your husband.'

'I really don't like you objectifying my husband,' replied Daniel.

'Liar,' said Katy, knocking back some more vodka. 'You love it.'

'Don't let her join in,' Daniel said to Ruth. 'Can you imagine if she had to kiss me? I might never recover. The thought of it makes me feel sick.'

'You can all join in,' said Ruth. 'The more the merrier. Right, are we ready – off you go, Bridget.'

Bridget chucked the parcel at her neighbour, who passed it to her left, then the parcel flew over the back of a seat to the next row and it shuffled along until it was lobbed over another row and right into Daniel's lap just at the moment that Ruth shouted, 'Cock and Bull!'

'Ooh,' said Daniel, clapping his hands in excitement. He handed his drink to Katy and began to rip off the paper. Into his lap fell a chocolate penis lollipop.

'Oh,' said Ruth. 'I forgot I put those in.'

'You all need to sit down,' shouted a steward walking up the gangway.

'I'm so sorry,' apologised Ruth, turning a charming smile on the man bearing down on them.

'I need you all in your seats and belted up,' he continued.

'Bit harsh,' muttered Daniel.

'It's for safety,' said the steward, glaring at Daniel. 'And may I remind you that the consumption of duty-free alcohol is strictly forbidden on board flights,' he continued, glaring at Daniel who now also had the bottle in his hand after it had done the rounds.

'Someone get out of bed the wrong side this morning?' said Daniel, stifling a giggle.

'I'm just trying to do my job,' he said.

'And you are doing an excellent job of offering five-star hospitality aboard this luxury flight,' replied Daniel. 'Would you like a lollipop?' He held the phallic sweet up in the steward's face.

'Could I ask you to put that away?'

Daniel giggled like a teenager caught doing something they shouldn't on the back of the school bus.

'I've got my eye on you,' said the steward, nodding at Daniel. 'Any funny business and I'll have the police waiting at the other end.'

'What!' said Daniel, outraged. 'What have I done? All I want to do is get through this flight any way I can so I can enjoy my holiday with my husband and my child and these two other lovely families that I'm going away with. And you're threatening to get me arrested.'

'You're not with this lot?' asked the steward, indicating those in the sparkling cowboy hats.

'No! We've only just met but I have to say they have been a damn sight more hospitable than you have so far. I may be writing to this airline and complimenting them on the standard of their customers but not of their staff. These people have given me free alcohol and snacks which I understand that unlike most civilised airlines you do not.' He pushed the bottle of vodka and the penis lollipop into the face of the steward yet again.

The man looked like he was ready to burst. He leaned forward until his head was at the same height as Daniel's head. He grabbed the vodka bottle and the lollipop out of his hands.

'You can have these back at the end of the flight,' he said. 'And like I said, I'm watching you.' He straightened and walked towards the back of the plane.

'But they're not mine,' Daniel shouted after him. 'Bring back their vodka and cockpop!'

Several other passengers looked up and stared, tutting as they did so.

He turned round and sank back into his chair.

'Just calm down, will you,' said Katy.

'He just took them off me,' he told her incredulously. 'I'm so sorry,' he said, turning to Ruth.

Ruth just shrugged. 'No bother. I've had worse flights. We forgot to get the duty-free at all once.'

'Let me buy you all a drink to compensate,' said Daniel.

'Are you mad? It'll cost a fortune,' replied Ruth.

'Least I can do,' muttered Daniel, reaching into his pocket for his wallet. 'Now, what are you drinking? Shall we see if we can drain them of vodka before we land?'

Chapter Six

'How you all doing over here?' asked Braindead, appearing in the aisle next to Abby forty-five minutes after they had taken off. Ruth had made everyone move around after take-off, which had delighted Abby as she was now sat next to two girls called Fi and Rachel who were an absolute scream. She couldn't believe how well this holiday was starting.

'We thought we'd come and say hello, didn't we, little chap?' Logan was walking between Braindead's legs, grasping both of his hands.

'Great,' nodded Abby vigorously. 'This is Fi,' she said, turning to her left. 'She's on a hen do with Cassie. They've been sharing their vodka with us,' she giggled, raising her cup up to show him.

'Oh,' said Braindead. 'Great. Glad you've found someone to talk to. Logan is loving flying but Millie has thrown up twice and Silvie won't stop crying.'

'You on a hen do as well?' asked Fi, lurching forward. 'Is it drunk crying or emotional crying? Happens on most hen dos. But not normally this early into the trip. Usually by day two someone will be a screwed-up mess in a toilet of a tequila bar, telling anyone who will listen that she is never going to get married and no-one loves her.'

Braindead stared back at her. 'Millie is five and ate too many sweets at the airport. Silvie is a baby and it's her first flight. I don't think she likes airline food,' he told Fi.

'This is my husband,' explained Abby.

'And this is our son Logan,' announced Braindead, picking up his son so Fi could have a better view. 'Say hello, Logan.'

Logan gurgled.

'Man,' said Fi to Abby. 'You never said you had a kid. You don't look old enough.'

'Well, thank you,' grinned Abby. 'Very kind of you to say so.' She raised her paper cup and took a swig of vodka.

'So, are you okay over here?' asked Braindead. 'I can swap if you want, if you want to sit with Logan?'

'No,' said Abby quickly, shaking her head. 'You're fine. Seriously, I'm okay here.'

'Right,' said Braindead, nodding slowly. 'Well, as long as you're all right. We'll go back to our seats. Say bye-bye Mummy,' he said, pointing Logan towards Abby. Abby leant forward and gave him a peck on the cheek.

'See you soon,' she said, giving him a little wave.

*

Katy had found herself sitting next to the bride-to-be and the tumbling of vodka down her throat had led her to offer all the wisdom she could muster on marriage and weddings to the learner wife.

'Ours was a lovely wedding,' she told Cassie. 'But if I had my time again then I'd do it like you. You know, in the right order for a start,' said Katy to the wide-eyed young woman as they continued to graze on neat alcohol. 'I hate telling people that we got married after we had Millie. You can see that look on their faces – you know, "Oh, so you had to get married then," that's what they're thinking, but it wasn't like that at all. We didn't plan Millie but she has been the best thing that has ever happened to us and when Ben proposed in the labour ward, well, you can't get more romantic than that, can you? I mean, I looked my absolute worst! Naked from the waist down, bodily fluids everywhere, a belly the size of Africa. It can't have been pretty and yet he wanted to marry me. Amazing, really.'

'How soon did you get married after that?' Cassie asked Katy.

'Oh well, it took a while and well… er, well, in the end I sprung a surprise wedding on him but that's a whole other story.'

'A surprise wedding?'

'Yeah, relationships are complicated, aren't they? You see, to cut a very long story short, I had a one-night stand not long after we got together and, well, as you can imagine it caused complications, but we're all good now. Never been better, in fact. Two kids, homeowners, jobs, solid as a rock we are. It was a rocky start but, you know, we were meant to be together. We've had tough times but I always knew we were destined.'

'How?' asked Cassie.

'What do you mean, how?'

'How did you know?'

'You just know.'

'But how?'

Katy let out a long sigh and took a large swig of her drink.

'It's just a feeling,' she said eventually. 'A feeling that overrides all your worries and concerns. That's how you know.'

Cassie didn't say anything, just stared into space.

'How did you meet your fiancé?' Katy asked her eventually.

'We had a one-night stand,' she said.

'Really!' said Katy.

'Well, I didn't know it was a one-night stand until I found out he had a girlfriend so I refused to see him again,' Cassie added. 'Then he dumped her for me and she tracked me down. Said he was the love of her life so I had better be worth it. That was three years ago. We got engaged last year on New Year's Eve in Paris. He already had the ring. It was his grandmother's. It's a sapphire.'

'So you are the opposite of me,' replied Katy after she had looked at Cassie's ring, considered Cassie's story and drunk some more vodka. 'You stuck with the man you had a one-night stand with whereas I didn't.'

'I guess you could say that's right,' replied Cassie.

They sat in silence for a moment.

'Does your husband worry that you might have a one-night stand again? You know, because you did it once already?' asked Cassie.

'No!' cried Katy. 'No, I'm sure he doesn't. It was a one-off. I'm not a cheater. Ben knows that.'

'Right,' said Cassie, gazing down into her paper cup.

'Anyway, we shouldn't be having this conversation now, it's your hen party! You don't need to be listening to me blithering on. You need to let your hair down. Have fun. That's the downside of throwing a surprise wedding. You don't get to have a hen party. I kind of regret that so you need to make the most of it.'

'You should join us,' said Cassie. 'Come out with us one night.'

Katy shook her head and laughed. 'No, I'm way too old for all that kind of stuff now. It's a lovely thought, but no.'

'Oh please,' said Cassie, looking slightly desperate. 'I... I'm a bit scared of what they're going to do to me.'

Katy looked at her in shock. 'But they're your friends. You'll be fine.'

'I know,' replied Cassie. 'But they go a bit wild and, well, it's just not me. I wanted to go and stay at a National Trust property and do one of those behind-the-scenes tours – you know, when you learn about the real history of the place and drink sherry. I suggested it to Ruth and she said she'd never heard anything so ridiculous in her life.'

Katy felt sorry for Cassie. Fortunately when all Katy's friends got married, hen parties had still largely been about doing what the hen wanted, whereas these days that didn't seem to be the case. It seemed to be all about who could plan the most outrageous holiday possible.

'Ruth is unstoppable,' continued Cassie. 'If I get home in one piece it will be a miracle. The store where we work couldn't open once after a hen do because so many people rang in sick.'

'You'll be fine,' said Katy, patting her hand whilst thinking she was so glad she was too old to go on hen parties any more. 'Just drink plenty of water.'

'Well, if you change your mind,' said Cassie, reaching into her bag and pulling out her phone. 'I'll give you my number, just in case you fancy a break from the kids one night?'

Now that did sound vaguely tempting, thought Katy.

Chapter Seven

'How many hours have we been on this coach now?' asked Daniel.

'It's a sixty-minute transfer time,' replied Katy. Then she whispered in his ear. 'Have you got any paracetamol? I think I can feel a headache coming on.'

'Here,' said Daniel, shoving a packet into her palm. 'I've just had two. I should know better than to drink vodka on a plane next to a woman called Ruth. She was a really bad influence. I cannot tell you right now how much I need ice-cold water and a darkened room.'

'Do you think the guys spotted that we had a bit too much to drink on the plane?' asked Katy.

'Gabriel is a saint, as we all know, and smiled at me as we got off the plane in an "aren't I lucky to have a crazy mad English husband who makes friends with hen party on a plane" kind of way.'

'Ben gave me a stern look so I grabbed Millie and Jack and told him he was a saint,' replied Katy. 'He said he knew and was looking forward to me being up in the night with Jack.'

'Braindead looked kind of oblivious when Abby fell down the stairs of the plane,' said Daniel, raising his eyebrows. 'Good job she was drunk or else that could have been nasty. She's fast asleep now, look. She's going to feel like death when she wakes up. I cannot wait to lie down. What with the early start and the early hangover, all I want to do is go to sleep.'

*

'I am not sleeping in that,' announced Daniel when he finally saw his room some time later. 'Is it because we are gay?' he asked Gabriel. 'Is that why they have done this? Is this what they do these days? These passive-aggressive little protests designed to make us feel like second-class citizens. Is this what we are up against?'

'You have a hangover. You need to calm down,' said Gabriel.

'I do not need to calm down, it's just not right. They cannot do this to us.'

'It is just twin beds, Daniel. It is not the end of the world. You can survive for one week.'

'But… but… I come on holiday to be close to you, not look at you across six yards of chipped white tiles.'

'Then we shall push the beds together. See, it is easy. Not a problem. Now are you going to unpack or bath Silvie?'

Daniel knew he should bath Silvie. Gabriel had taken care of her all day without any protest. He sighed. This was going to hurt.

'I'll bath her,' he said, holding out his arms and taking her from Gabriel. He held his breath. She could smell his fear, he was sure. He carried her through to the bathroom. The minute he shut the door the wailing began and for the second time that day he regretted ever meeting Ruth as his head throbbed with a daytime hangover.

*

'Ring them again,' said Katy, pacing the room.

'But I only rang ten minutes ago,' said Ben, lying back on the bed and looking very interested in the Spanish soap opera that was on the TV.

'But they aren't doing anything, are they?' she shrieked. This was a disaster of epic proportions. She had been so clear when they had booked the holiday what was required. What were they going to do if they didn't resolve this? Absolutely no-one would be getting any sleep whatsoever. They would be returning home as zombies.

'I'm going down to reception,' she said at last. 'Whoever is answering the phone clearly doesn't realise the seriousness of the situation.'

'Okay,' shrugged Ben.

Clearly Ben did not understand the seriousness of the situation either. Or was it just that he wasn't suffering with a hangover like she was, and therefore was dealing with the issues of ensuring their room was a safe, calm environment for them to be in for the week much better than her?

It had started with the balcony. She'd checked that it had a child lock on the sliding door that accessed it and then had a fit when she discovered that there were chairs and a table dangerously close to the rail. Millie or Jack could have climbed onto them and then jumped off the balcony and died! Ben had told her to calm down but she refused until he had removed the table and chairs from said balcony and now they were cluttering up the already quite tight room.

Then there had been no plug for the bath. How on earth was she supposed to bath two children without a plug? A plug in a bath wasn't too much to ask, was it?

But that wasn't the worst of it. Having discovered the lack of plug, she then realised that there were only two double beds in the room. They were missing the cot they had been promised for Jack and that was essential for their sanity. The cot that would keep him out of danger and out of their bed whilst they slept. There was no way they could deal with this holiday without a cot.

It was after eight o'clock when Katy walked up to the reception desk, trying to stay calm. Her headache was just about at its peak and she was so tired, she could have cried.

'We were promised a cot,' she blurted out to the first person who became free behind the desk. She was ready for them to say they had run out, at which point she would kill someone.

The lady looked blank for a moment.

'We were promised a cot and we don't have one in our room,' Katy said.

'Which room, madam?'

'Room 204.'

The lady tapped at a computer. Katy poised ready to pounce should she give the wrong answer.

'I am sorry, madam,' she said looking up. 'I will call housekeeping and have them send one up to you.'

Katy took a breath. She had been ready for this answer as well.

'My husband has called twice in the last hour and both times been promised that a cot is on its way and it has not arrived.'

The lady looked back at her steadily. She picked up a phone and spoke rapidly in Spanish. She put the phone down.

'Our porters are all busy transferring luggage but there should be one free in half an hour and they will be asked to get a cot to you immediately.'

Half an hour. Half an hour before she could lie down and switch off.

Katy leant forward on the desk and stared at the woman behind it.

'Do you have children?' she asked.

'No,' replied the woman.

'When you have children,' she began, 'you will understand that half an hour can be a very, very, very long time. Imagine listening to someone scrape their fingernails down a blackboard for half an hour. That is the equivalent of the last half hour before you know you can put your children to bed. The clock literally slows down before your eyes, never has time gone slower. In fact, I truly believe that the world stops, yes, stops, whilst you are waiting to put your children to bed, so that finally for the first time that day you can hear yourself fucking think!'

She paused for what she hoped was dramatic effect.

'If that cot is not in our room within the next ten minutes I will be down here and I will sit here and scratch my fingernails down that charming little blackboard you have perched on this desk telling me that the weather today has been amazing but tomorrow it will be cloudy with a chance of showers until my husband calls me and tells me that the cot is in the bedroom and my son is in said cot. Do you understand?'

The lady nodded grimly but didn't move. Katy looked pointedly down at the phone and waited until she had picked it up and was dialling a number before she turned round and walked wearily back to the lift.

*

'Ben's on the phone,' said Braindead to Abby, who was lying on the bed with a wet flannel over her forehead. 'Wants to know if we have a cot for Logan in our room?'

Without opening her eyes Abby pointed to the cot that was plainly sitting in the corner.

'Yes, mate, we have,' said Braindead. He went quiet for a minute.

'Well, you can borrow ours if one doesn't turn up. We've got two beds in here. Logan can bunk up with one of us if need be.'

Abby began to shake her head vigorously.

'Well, he can bunk up with me at least,' he continued. 'No bother. Right, see you in the morning, mate, but let me know if you need the cot.'

He put the phone down, chuckling.

'Katy's downstairs apparently ripping the head off the receptionist because they haven't put a cot in the room for Jack, and Millie's kicking off because she hadn't realised that there wouldn't be Disney Junior on the TV in the hotel room. She says Spain is the worst country she's ever been to. Ben actually sounds a bit stressed. The joy of two kids, I suppose.'

Abby said nothing. Braindead watched her chest rise and fall.

'Must be nice though,' he said as he settled himself next to Abby on the bed with Logan in his arms. 'When you know you've completed your family and they're all well and that and you've got the next eighteen years to enjoy them, touch wood. Always felt a bit sorry for those who have twins or triplets because it's all condensed, isn't it? You're not stretching it or anything. They're born and you go through it all at the same time. No thinking, well, when one leaves at least I'll have the other one for a few years longer. Mind you, I guess if you have triplets then you only need to go through pregnancy and childbirth the once, which I imagine would be quite appealing. So would you rather have triplets and get it all over with or be pregnant and give birth three separate times?'

Abby didn't answer.

'Abby, did you hear me?' said Braindead, turning towards her. 'Would you rather have triplets or be pregnant three times—'

'Yes, I heard you,' said Abby, suddenly pulling herself up on her elbows. 'And the answer is no!' She got off the bed and staggered into the bathroom, slamming the door behind her.

'Oh,' said Braindead, looking down at Logan. 'Looks like you'll only be getting one more brother or sister,' he told him. He kissed the top of his head. 'But we might change her mind, hey?' he added. 'We might even persuade her to have a football team. You never know.'

Chapter Eight

'Where's Abby?' asked Ben the following day, plonking himself down on a sun lounger next to Braindead.

'Still in bed,' replied Braindead. 'Fast asleep, haven't got a word out of her. Even the words "buffet breakfast" didn't seem to have any impact. I mean, how can you ignore those two words? It's like a dream come true, mate. Best two words in the English language, I reckon. Me and Logan have been down and thoroughly indulged. Well, I did. Full English plus two pancakes and three rounds of toast. I made sure Logan was healthy though. Yoghurt, fruit and one slice of toast for him. You need to set a good example, don't you?'

'Very wise,' said Ben, leaning back on his chair and shading his eyes against the sun.

'So where's Katy and the kids?' asked Braindead.

'She took them both to the play area,' he said with a small smile. 'She's feeling guilty for getting drunk on the plane yesterday so is bending over backwards to make up for it. Although I think she might be regretting it, judging by the unholy racket that was coming from the playground. Not the greatest place to be with a hangover. How's Abby's head? She was pretty wrecked yesterday. Did she get a bruise from that fall?'

Braindead shrugged. 'No idea. She barely said a word after we got into the hotel room. Just went to bed. I suggested a walk on the beach at some point but she just groaned and rolled over. She missed seeing Logan's face when he first put his toes in the water. She'll regret that. Still, I took loads of pictures.'

'You, mate, are hilarious,' came a voice from behind them followed by a giggle from Logan.

Braindead and Ben whipped their heads round to find Logan pouring water all over the feet of a man lying on a sunbed behind them.

'Oh God, mate, I'm sorry,' said Braindead, leaping up and grabbing his son under the armpits. 'Logan, what do you think you're doing?'

'It's all right,' said the man, who must have been in his mid-twenties and had a very round rosy-cheeked face that clearly wasn't friends with the sun. 'He's fine, I'm not bothered. I've got twin nieces who have done far worse.'

'Twins!' said Braindead. 'Wow. I was only saying last night how insane twins would be. This is Logan, by the way, who has already tried to ruin your holiday, and I'm his dad Craig, but call me Braindead because everyone else does, and this is my mate Ben.'

'Hi,' said Ben, holding his hand out to shake.

'Hi,' the man replied, grasping Ben's hand. 'I'm Ollie.'

'You here with your kids then?' asked Ben.

'No,' replied Ollie, suddenly looking a bit uncomfortable. 'Actually I'm here on my own.'

'Really!' exclaimed Braindead. 'How come?'

'Well, er, I...' began Ollie, going bright red.

Oh goodness, thought Ben. Logan had found a freak to play with.

'Well, I should have been coming with my wife,' spluttered out Ollie, 'but, er... well... she called off the wedding a month ago. Too late to cancel so I thought I'd just come anyway.'

'So you're on your honeymoon, right now, *alone*?' asked Braindead in awe.

'And now you know why we call him Braindead all the time,' said Ben. 'Tact is not his strong point.'

'Well, he's right,' said Ollie. 'Although I hadn't quite pictured it like that in my head. I was trying to forget it should have been my honeymoon and treat it just as a holiday.'

'A holiday, yes, of course, a holiday,' said Braindead. 'Who mentioned honeymoon? I didn't mention honeymoon. Are you in the honeymoon suite?'

'Braindead!' cried Ben. 'Not helpful.'

They both paused, waiting for Ollie to answer.

'Yes, I am,' he said eventually.

'Jesus,' said Braindead. 'That's got to hurt.'

'I did tell them that it would just be me coming,' said Ollie. 'That it was no longer a honeymoon but when I opened the door to the room there was—'

'Don't tell me, the bed had a heart-shaped sprinkling of rose petals, there were candles lit and two swans made out of towels in the centre of the bed with their necks entwined,' interrupted Braindead.

'How did you know?' gasped Ollie.

'I came to Spain on honeymoon two years ago. It was quite possibly the most romantic thing I had ever seen and I cried, but I had just got married,' he replied.

Ollie looked at them and swallowed. 'I cried,' he spluttered.

'Because you had to sleep all alone in a petal-strewn bed,' said Braindead. 'Of course you cried. And it's really difficult to unfurl those swan-towel things. That's enough to make you cry.'

Ollie dropped his head for a moment. Ben and Braindead looked at each other.

'It's all right, mate,' said Ben. 'Braindead here didn't manage to have sex on his honeymoon if that makes you feel any better.'

'Ben!' said Braindead.

'I'm just trying to cheer the man up,' said Ben.

'It's a very long story,' said Braindead after Ollie had raised his head with a shocked expression.

'A very long story,' agreed Ben.

'But we're all sorted now,' Braindead continued. 'Look,' he said, pointing at Logan, who was bringing another bucket of water back towards them from the pool. 'Even managed to produce this little terrorist.'

'Lucky you,' said Ollie, looking wistfully at Logan. He sighed deeply. 'To be honest, I thought I'd be sitting here talking about when we were going to start a family,' he said. 'You're a lucky man. Where's your wife then?'

'She's, er… having a lie-in.'

'I bet,' replied Ollie. 'Having kids is exhausting, isn't it? Well, I told you about my sister. All parents deserve a lie-in.'

'Yeah,' said Braindead.

'My wife's down the playground with our two,' said Ben. 'She had too much to drink on the plane yesterday and so it's a guilt trip,' he grinned. 'But I'm not complaining.'

'So when did you arrive?' asked Braindead.

'Oh, last week. I'm over half way through now.'

'Wow,' gasped Braindead. 'What have you been doing?'

'Well, I've read a lot. I took myself down the waterfront a couple of nights, you know, to try and mingle, but no-one wants to talk to a guy on his own. It's like I've got a big flag with "Loser" written above my head. This group of girls took pity on me for a bit but when I explained I should have been on my honeymoon they got a bit weirded out and so they dumped me. Not that I've ever been any good at talking to women. I mean, my sister says I'm appalling. I just can't do it, I've never had to chat a girl up in my life.'

'But you must have chatted up your fiancée?' asked Ben.

'We'd been together since we were fourteen,' Ollie explained. 'We used to walk home from school together and then she asked me to go to McDonald's with her and then kind of assumed we were girlfriend and boyfriend.'

'Fourteen!' exclaimed Braindead. 'Are you serious? Are you telling me that you have never had another girlfriend apart from the woman who dumped you four weeks before your wedding day?'

'Braindead!' said Ben, 'you really need to work on how you phrase things.'

Ben turned to look at Ollie, who admitted that Braindead was correct in his assumption.

'You are practically a virgin!' announced Braindead.

'Braindead!' said Ben. 'Please!'

'It's all right,' said Ollie, shaking his head sadly.

They sat in silence for a few moments contemplating Ollie's fate whilst Logan poured water over his feet.

'Is that bothering you?' said Braindead eventually, pointing at his son.

'It's fine,' said Ollie. 'Worse has happened to me recently.'

'Better off out of it, I reckon,' said Braindead. 'I mean, I've never met this woman but you need to experience some life, man. Have some fun. Get out and go wild or something.'

'Yeah, well maybe,' replied Ollie.

'I've just thought of something,' said Ben, starting to laugh.

'You can't laugh,' said Braindead. 'And you think I'm insensitive!'

'I was just thinking about if you pulled here and it went really well and you invited a girl back to your room and you open the door and it's the… honeymoon suite!'

'Christ! What would she think?' added Braindead. 'There's no way she'd believe it. Dumped at the altar… I don't think so. More likely you've come on holiday with your new wife and bumped her off because you'd already had enough.'

'This holiday is doomed, isn't it?' said Ollie. 'I'm not sure why I even came. Maybe I should get an early flight home and cut my losses.'

'You could say that you're just that kind of guy,' continued Ben, oblivious to Ollie's discomfort. 'That wherever you stay, you just have to have the best room, which in this hotel happens to be the honeymoon suite.'

'Then she'd just think you were a twat and run a mile,' said Braindead. 'No, I think Ollie is right. This honeymoon is doomed.'

They sat in awkward silence, feeling Ollie's pain but not knowing what to say about it. Thankfully Daniel arrived just in time to offer yet another opinion to the poor single honeymooner.

'So this is where you're all hiding,' he said, resplendent in linen. 'Well, you two at least. Hello, I'm Daniel,' he said, sticking his hand out to shake Ollie's. 'And this is my husband Gabriel and our daughter Silvie,' he continued, turning to introduce the rest of the family behind him.

'I'm Ollie,' said Ollie.

'Ollie's not on his honeymoon,' announced Braindead.

Daniel pulled down his sunglasses and peered over the top of them. 'Dumped at the altar?' he asked.

Ollie gasped. 'Not quite. Four weeks before actually.'

Daniel nodded.

'How could you tell?' asked Braindead.

'I noticed as we approached that his back is burned, indicating that he is holidaying alone and has no-one to ask to apply sun lotion. He is wearing this season's Ralph Lauren swimming shorts and yet I suspect he doesn't normally wear designer labels so it is clear he should be here on a special occasion, however he is clearly not, given the sad doleful puppy-eyed look on his face. My condolences, young man,' he said. 'But better to have ended before the marriage was cemented rather than suffer years of mediocrity until she found someone who shuffled her away. Was there anyone else involved, by the way? I assume there was.'

'No!' said Ollie. 'No, she said not.'

'There will have been. It will all come out in about a month's time when she believes the dust has settled and it will hurt you less but of course it will hurt more as you will then know that she had been lying to you all along.'

'Bloody hell, Daniel,' said Ben. 'So glad to have the angel of doom on holiday with us.'

'Do you really think so?' Ollie asked Daniel, his face drained of colour despite the rosy burnt glow on his cheeks.

'I would bet my new Calvin Klein sunglasses on it,' said Daniel, carefully laying down a towel on a sun lounger. 'There are few that are brave enough to walk into the abyss of singledom without someone to hold their hand, even it is just temporary. Many a mediocre marriage has been avoided by the arrival of a mediocre third party. The good news is that she is unlikely to stay with him. She just needed someone to help her jump ship. Once she's out there and can see that she's survived then she'll cast him aside as he has done his job.'

Ollie stared at Daniel with his mouth open.

'But she said that she had just fallen out of love with me,' he said. 'She promised me that there was no-one else involved.'

'Well,' said Daniel, 'if that's what you want to believe, you just carry on, but I'm usually right on these things.'

'Ella Jefferson told me straight when she dumped me,' butted in Braindead. 'She said when I kissed her she found herself thinking about what she was going to have for tea but when Clive Dixon kissed her all she could think about was Patrick Swayze. I think she married him in the end.'

'What, Patrick Swayze?' asked Ben.

'No, Clive Dixon.'

'Do you think she still thinks about Patrick Swayze?'

'I've no idea,' replied Braindead.

'Lucky escape there, I reckon,' said Ben.

'Exactly,' said Braindead, looking over at Ollie, who still looked like he was reeling in shock at Daniel's view on the crashing of his nuptials. 'It's all for the best,' he told him. 'Imagine if Clive Dixon hadn't come along. I could be married to someone who reminded her of fish fingers when I kissed her.'

Ollie didn't reply. In fact he looked overwhelmed by the input from the group that he had just befriended.

'You need to get out there and enjoy yourself,' said Daniel, taking hold of Silvie on his knee whilst Gabriel rubbed sun cream into her legs.

'You need a nice Spanish girl,' added Gabriel, smiling at him. 'For holiday romance.'

'He's been out,' said Braindead. 'Everyone thinks he's a loser because he's on his own so won't talk to him.'

'And he's got the honeymoon suite,' added Ben. 'Guaranteed to freak out any potential love interest.'

'You have the honeymoon suite!' exclaimed Daniel, taking his glasses off and staring at Ollie.

Ollie nodded. 'I hate it,' he replied numbly.

'We'll take it,' said Daniel. 'We'll have it. Can you believe that they've given us single beds, the cheek of it? We'll swap with you.'

'Whoa, whoa, whoa,' said Braindead. 'You can't do that. You've only just met. He's our friend. We'll take it. It might remind Abby of our honeymoon. They'd let us put a cot in there, wouldn't they, for Logan?'

'Do you have a double bed in your room?' asked Daniel, handing Silvie to Gabriel and standing up with his hands on his hips.

'Yes, we do,' nodded Braindead.

'Then me and Gabriel should have the honeymoon suite. We have single beds. It's not right. They have made a terrible mistake.'

'Then you have our double bed,' said Braindead, 'and me and Abby will have the honeymoon suite. Then everyone's happy.'

'But why should you get the honeymoon suite and not us?' said Daniel.

'Because we saw him first,' replied Braindead. 'We've been cheering him up for ages and then you just steam in and think that you can steal his bed. That's not fair, is it?'

'Don't you think you should ask Ollie if he wants to give up his luxury suite with Jacuzzi and balcony overlooking the sea?' interrupted Ben.

'There's a Jacuzzi!' exclaimed Braindead and Daniel.

'I've no idea,' replied Ben. 'I just made that up. Is there, Ollie?'

Ollie nodded. 'And a balcony overlooking the sea,' he added.

'Look, I'll pay you,' said Daniel, taking a step towards the poor lad. 'I'll pay you to swap rooms with us.'

'That's so unfair,' declared Braindead. 'I can't afford to pay him and you know that,' he argued, prodding Daniel's shoulder with his finger.

'Don't prod me,' said Daniel, prodding back.

'I will if you are using dirty tactics,' replied Braindead, prodding him again.

'If you touch me again…' said Daniel, giving Braindead a shove.

'Lads, come on, calm down,' said Ben, getting up to intervene. 'You're behaving like children.'

Braindead looked at Ben and then leant forward and gave Daniel an almighty shove, causing him to stagger back and fall into the pool behind him.

'Oh my God,' gasped Braindead in surprise, dashing to the side of the pool and reaching in to pull him out. 'I'm so sorry,' he gasped. 'I didn't mean that to happen.'

Daniel flailed around reaching out for Braindead's hand then tugged him sharply, causing Braindead to tumble into the water too.

Ben and Gabriel stood and laughed at the pair as they splashed back towards the edge of the pool.

'Are you two going to grow up now?' Ben asked them as they hauled themselves out. 'Leave Ollie and his suite alone, eh?' he added. 'He's traumatised enough as it is without you causing him extra stress.'

'No, I mean, I'd be happy to swap with someone actually…' began Ollie.

'Don't say it,' said Ben, clamping his hand on his shoulder. 'Don't breathe a word. We could have World War Three if you're not careful. No, you keep your luxury honeymoon suite and we'll all cope with sharing a room with the wriggliest, noisiest, most demanding human beings you can imagine. We'll be absolutely fine.'

Chapter Nine

By the time Katy got to the pool with Jack and Millie some time later, she was a nervous wreck.

'Hi,' she said, looking flustered as she dumped down two enormous bags overflowing with towels and pool toys. 'Sorry but I lost Jack for a whole fifteen minutes only to find him playing *in* the lift. I didn't know whether to hug him or kill him.'

'I got to number ten,' said Jack proudly to his dad.

'Wow,' said Ben, holding his hand up to high five before Katy glared at him.

'And Millie has already got her Elsa outfit caught on the slide and ripped it and I told her not to wear it to the playground but she insisted and now she's all upset because it's ruined and can't understand why I don't want to go to a shop immediately and buy a new one,' continued Katy, sitting down and putting her head in her hands.

'I promised Elsa she could come on holiday with us and now I'll have to leave her behind in the room so we have to go and buy a new Elsa,' Millie explained to Ben. 'We shouldn't break promises, should we, Daddy? If we don't get a new Elsa, I will have broken my promise and I will be a bad person.'

'Look,' he said. 'Let's go in the pool, shall we? Elsa wouldn't be able to go in there anyway so let's worry about her later after we've been in the pool.'

'Why wouldn't Elsa be able to go in the pool?' asked Millie.

Ben glanced at Katy, who still had her head in her hands.

'Because she can't swim,' he replied.

Millie gasped.

'Why can't she swim?'

'Because they didn't teach girls to swim in the olden days,' he replied.

'Why not?'

'Because princesses didn't need to know how to swim, they were too busy being princesses.'

Millie stared at him for a moment trying to process this piece of information.

'Then we must teach her how to swim,' she eventually concluded.

Katy groaned. She could so tell where this was going. She had already been back up to the room twice to fetch forgotten items, which was no mean feat when also marshalling two dawdling children.

Ben had gone quiet. She daren't raise her head and look at him for fear that then she would be forced to collude on how to solve the current crisis.

'Before you can teach Elsa, don't you think you need to practise?' said Ben. 'Make sure you can do it properly so you can teach her properly.'

Nice one, thought Katy, daring to raise her head. Her daughter had her face screwed up thinking this through and eventually agreed that perhaps that was an acceptable answer.

'You'll have to come in if they are both coming in,' Ben told Katy. 'I don't think I can keep hold of both of them.'

Katy looked down at the sun lounger and thought of her book in her bag, so near and yet so far. She stood up and, with the air of someone preparing to be hanged, slowly took off the enormous piece of floaty fabric which was doing a grand job of hiding her wobbly bits.

She stood in her one-piece swimsuit which didn't quite fit and was a startling pink print because she'd left it too late to go shopping and so all the good swimsuits had gone. It would be a low point in any scenario, unsuitably dressed and about to charter tricky waters and with the nagging thought at the back of her head that this also meant she would have to wash and dry her hair later. Her heart filled with resignation rather than relaxation, which would be preferable on the first day of one's holiday.

*

Pool time with kids could have been enjoyable had it not been for the constant splashing in the face with water, or pulling of hair or kicking of tiny feet against the belly or digging of tiny fingernails in the arm or the constant terror that you might lose concentration and they might drown. Apart from that it was an absolute delight and Katy was so glad that they had all agreed that a pool was essential for a successful summer holiday with kids.

Eventually the children grew tired. Millie started crying because Jack kicked her in the face and so they all agreed that pool time was over. Finally Katy got to put her bottom on a sun lounger as she dried Millie and wondered whether she had the energy to insist that they both needed another layer of sunscreen or if that would spark a tirade of complaints that she wasn't sure she could deal with.

She was hoping that now might be her chance for maybe ten minutes with her book but she hadn't worked out her strategy for achieving this. Perhaps she should suggest that Ben take them to the games room but this hardly seemed fair on him. Perhaps if she offered to take them Ben might insist he take them as he loved a games room, but it was a high-risk strategy that could end up with her alone in a windowless room with two children demanding extortionate amounts of money to fritter away on pointless machines.

She reached in her bag to check the time on her phone. Maybe it was time to send off Ben, Jack and Millie to check out the lunch options, which might afford just a few minutes' respite.

To her surprise there was a missed call and three texts awaiting her from Cassie, the reluctant hen party bride.

Hiya – hope you are having a good first day. Just in case you have changed your mind we will all be in Larry's Bar which I think is down the road from your hotel tomorrow night. Would love you to come. Cassie x

Katy shook her head. It was tempting. More tempting than yesterday given the morning that she'd had. It could be her only chance of something resembling a holiday experience.

8pm by the way. We'll be dressed up but come as you are. C x

Katy shook her head again. Hen party alarm bells went off in her head. Dressing up? Even if she didn't have to, she was way too old to be around people who did.

Please come xx

Katy furrowed her brow at the last text. Kind of desperate sounding. But no, it was a bad idea. She hadn't come on holiday to go out and get drunk, she'd come on holiday for a lovely family time. She threw her phone back in her bag, deciding that she would text back later and politely decline.

'Should we think about lunch?' she announced to her fellow happy holidaymakers. Daniel of course was stretched out on a lounger somehow managing to read a book whilst Silvie nestled between Gabriel's legs and chewed on her own cloth book. Braindead had made his towel into a hillside landscape for Logan's cars and they were busy driving them round complete with engine noises. There was still no sign of Abby.

'Good thinking,' said Braindead, looking up. 'I clearly didn't have enough buffet at the buffet breakfast. I'm starving.'

'I saw a lovely little tapas bar in the next town when we drove past yesterday from the airport,' piped up Daniel. 'The specials board outside said squid and gazpacho. Two of my favourites. Why don't we all go there?'

Katy looked at him as though he was out of his mind.

'Are you out of your mind?' she asked him.

Daniel blinked back. 'No,' he replied. 'I'm merely trying to make a suggestion for lunch, that's all.'

'To a tapas bar!' she said. 'Miles away! Serving squid and cold soup?'

'It's merely in the next town, a short taxi ride away, and what is wrong with squid and cold soup?'

'Nothing,' she replied. 'Unless you're travelling with small children, making going to a restaurant in the next town entail a time-consuming trip back to the hotel room, where they will be most upset that you have made them take a bath and put on clean clothes and reapply sunscreen yet again before you gather all the necessary accoutrements to keep kids happy during a grown-up meal in a grown-up restaurant, including books they will not look at and games they will not play until they find the iPad that you have hidden in the bottom of your bag in case of emergencies, which you realise pretty soon after you arrive that you are actually in an emergency as you have taken them to a restaurant where they don't serve chips and nuggets, just squid or cold soup!'

Daniel waited a moment before he replied.

'I think you are seeing unnecessary barriers,' he said calmly.

'Fine,' she replied. 'You go. You go and enjoy your cold soup and squid.'

'Well, that hardly seems in the spirit of the holiday,' said Daniel. 'Where were you thinking?'

Katy sighed, not knowing what was more depressing, the thought of not going to the nice restaurant with the lovely squid and gazpacho or going where she was about to suggest.

'I just thought it would be easiest to order some hotdogs from the pool bar,' she muttered.

'Hotdogs!' exclaimed Daniel. 'You've dragged me all the way to Spain to eat hotdogs?'

'It's just easier,' she gasped. 'You know, with the kids,' she added, feeling as depressed as Daniel was no doubt feeling. 'You'll understand when Silvie is older. Easy always outweighs better when it comes to kids. Always.'

They stared at each other in a moment of dawning realisation that she was right.

'Will there be any moments of adult joy at all on this holiday?' asked Daniel.

Katy couldn't bear to answer him.

'Shall I go and order?' said Ben, getting up and hoisting Jack onto his hip. 'Hotdogs and chips all round, is it?'

'I suppose so,' muttered Daniel.

'Yes please,' also muttered Katy.

'Oh yes,' said Braindead. 'And a small one for this one and don't forget the ketchup. Lots of ketchup, please.'

'How about you, Ollie?' Ben shouted over to their new friend. 'Want to join us for lunch? We can't take you out on the town and pull women but we'll share a hotdog with you.'

'Well, that's very kind,' said Ollie. 'If you're sure. I'll come and help you.'

'Gabriel,' Ben finally asked. 'You up for some local delicacy known as *Las Hotas Dogas?*'

'If that is what you Brits choose to eat in Spain then yes, of course,' he replied, looking unusually glum. 'But I will wash mine down with some red wine in the true Spanish style if you don't mind.'

'Wow,' muttered Daniel, still clearly in a bad mood. 'That will make up for the gazpacho.'

'And here is Abby, just in time for lunch,' announced Ben, looking up and starting to clap. 'Did you smell the hotdogs, Abby?'

Katy looked up to see Abby walking towards them with a big grin on her face.

'Here she is!' Braindead exclaimed. 'Here's Mummy. She must be feeling better, eh? Logan and I made a new friend,' Braindead told her. 'This is Ollie.'

Abby glanced over but barely seemed to acknowledge him.

'Stop sucking up to Ollie,' said Daniel to Braindead. 'I know what you're up to.'

'Guess what?' said Abby, grinning from ear to ear. 'Fi from the hen party yesterday has sent a message asking if Katy, Daniel and I want to join them for a night out tomorrow night. I'm going to drink negronis and then we're going for tapas.'

'Yes!' cried out Daniel.

'*You* want to go out on a hen night?' said Katy incredulously.

'I've just been told that my main culinary highlights this week will be hotdogs and now Abby has arrived with news of cocktails and tapas. Of course I want to go.'

'Pool, Daddy?' Logan suddenly shouted. 'Pool now, Daddy.'

Braindead didn't answer, just stared at Abby.

'Mummy,' said Millie, tugging on her mum's hand. 'Can I have ice cream for lunch?'

'You'll come, won't you, Katy?' Abby asked her. 'Please come with me.'

'Well, I, er,' stuttered Katy. When she'd had the text from Cassie she had no desire to go but suddenly a night out without kids and with grown-ups and real food, not fast food, did sound very appealing.

'Daniel's coming, aren't you?' pressed Abby.

'Well, as long as it's okay with Gabriel?' he said, looking over at his husband.

No-one said anything.

'You should go,' said Gabriel. 'Look after Abby and Katy and have fun and the rest of us will be Daddy Day Care.' He paused. 'And to keep everyone happy and to make sure we *all* have fun then the next night maybe me and Ben and Braindead will take out Ollie here and show him a good time. Find him a beautiful Spanish lady, perhaps. How does that sound to everyone?'

Abby got up and dashed over to Gabriel and embraced him in a hug. 'What a brilliant idea,' she gasped. 'I thought this was going to be a terrible holiday, what with being stuck with the kids and everything, but it's going to be great!'

Ben watched Braindead's face fall.

'I suppose it's okay,' said Ben when no-one said anything. 'That is of course if that's what you want to do, Katy?'

Katy shrugged. It wasn't what she had expected for this holiday but Abby had already decided she was in the hen party gang and, actually, the more she got into this family holiday malarkey, the more a grown-ups-only night out sounded fun.

'I really don't want you to plan your holiday around me,' interjected Ollie, looking mortified. 'I mean, you're already letting me share hotdogs with you.'

Ben swiftly put his hand on Ollie's shoulder. 'It's fine,' he said. 'What do you think, Braindead?'

Braindead lifted Logan into his arms and kissed his forehead. 'If that's what everyone wants to do,' he said quietly, 'it's fine by me.'

'Great,' said Abby. 'I'll text Fi now. Tell her we're on. Then I really need to think of what I'm going to wear. Isn't this brilliant? I really feel like I'm on holiday now.'

Katy looked over at Ben. She had a bad feeling that the 'wives' getting involved in a hen party whilst the 'husbands' went out to try and fix up a jilted fiancé wasn't the answer to making this holiday go like a dream but it looked like that was where it was heading. Their holiday entertainment had been chosen and surprisingly, hers involved deely-bopper penises and ridiculous drinking games whilst her husband would be trawling the bars helping someone pick up women. This already felt like a family holiday gone seriously wrong and she could only hope that they would all get to the end of it intact.

Chapter Ten

Ben could see Daniel standing in reception as they came out of the lift and his heart sank. He had his hands on his hips and didn't look happy. Personally, Ben had been looking forward to dinner all afternoon. They'd selected an all-you-can-eat buffet in the hotel to keep things simple after the lunchtime debacle. It sounded like a meal made in heaven to Ben but Daniel clearly wasn't on the same page as him.

'Have you seen it?' he exclaimed as they walked towards him. Jack was in the pushchair in the vague hope that later he might climb in and fall asleep as they took a seat in the bar and enjoyed some adult time. Millie had had her hair plaited and insisted on wearing her now safety-pinned-together Elsa dress. It was looking really special teamed with a pair of black Crocs. Ben had put a book in the nappy bag for her to read quietly later. Well, that was the plan. He'd also put in an iPad and some headphones but he and Katy had agreed that this would be produced only as a last resort in order to keep them quiet. They weren't the type of parents who let their kids use electronics at the dinner table... often.

Daniel was looking immaculate in linen trousers and a pristine white T-shirt which was so clean it positively shone in a way that none of Ben's white clothes ever did. Optimistic to wear white, thought Ben. They were about to go into an all-you-can-eat buffet with four young children.

'Just look at this, will you,' urged Daniel as they reached them. 'I have seen some sights in my life but I have never ever seen anything quite like this.'

Ben looked to where he was indicating and indeed it was quite a shock. On one side of reception next to the entrance to the dining room there was what could only be described as a sea of pushchairs/buggies/scooters/kids' ride-ons. There must have been over fifty contraptions littering the pathway to their fine-ish dining experience.

'What is that?' asked Daniel, looking utterly perplexed.

'I think it's what's known as your version of hell,' grinned Ben.

'And they are all parked here because…' asked Daniel.

'Well, I guess it means that all the occupiers of those vehicles are in there,' said Ben, pointing to the restaurant.

Daniel visibly paled.

'There cannot be that many children all in one place,' he said.

'Surely you are used to kids since Silvie arrived?' asked Ben, pushing Jack towards the mechanical chaos and starting to unbuckle him from out of his pushchair.

'Silvie is of course the love of my life along with Gabriel, but other kids… no, I don't get it.'

'What about Millie and Jack and Logan?'

'Bearable,' replied Daniel matter of factly.

'Ow, thanks,' muttered Ben.

'No, I mean they're lovely, of course they are, but just because you have your own kid I don't get why it has to mean that you then have to spend so much time surrounded by other people's kids. I chose to have Silvie. I didn't choose to have some snotty-nosed kid who happens to go to a playgroup with her.'

'But you will want her to have friends, surely?'

Daniel looked over at Ben.

'I suppose so,' he replied, but he didn't look convinced.

'Shall we go in?' said Ben, lifting Jack into his arms.

Daniel gave a huge sigh and shrugged. 'Is this what being a parent is all about?' he asked. 'Continually having to lower your standards?'

'Maybe your standards were too high in the first place,' said Ben. 'Maybe what being a parent is all about is enjoying the simpler things in life, like a smile, or a giggle or being called Daddy, rather than a Michelin-starred meal or a designer suit.'

Daniel stared at Ben for some time. He swallowed and nodded.

'Into the fray we go then,' he said, taking a deep breath and stepping forward.

*

'I can only find two high chairs,' said Braindead, arriving back at the table they had nabbed by literally hovering for five minutes as they waited for a poor grandmother to finish. Katy was so quick to pull her chair from under her she had come close to upending the woman as she stood up.

'Put Silvie and Logan in them,' replied Ben. 'I'll go and get some food for Jack and there might be a chair free by then.'

'How can they not have enough high chairs?' questioned Katy. 'Surely that's a given in a hotel like this?'

'It'll be fine,' said Ben. 'Jack can sit on my knee if he has to.'

'Look!' cried Katy suddenly. 'That family are getting up over there, quick, look! They've got a high chair.'

Ben glanced across the room to a family of three. Mum, Dad and a baby of about a year old. They had a slew of empty plates in front of them and the dad was just leaning over to take the baby out. The mother had picked up her handbag and was rooting around in it. That high chair was his for the taking. Ben looked nervously around to see if anyone else had spotted it. He could see a family of five lingering by the door, waiting for a table to become free, the mother holding a baby in her arms who was bashing her over the head with a teething ring. The father had his eyes all over the restaurant, poised to jump the moment anyone showed any interest in leaving a table. Ben figured that perhaps he had only spotted that tables were in short supply and not high chairs. Perhaps Ben would be able to nip in and swoop the high chair away before the other father had had time to gather his wits about him and spot that getting a table for his brood was the least of his worries.

Ben began to walk across the room. Casually at first, so as not to draw attention, but then he felt himself speed up as the dad at the door spotted the impending availability of the table that Ben was targeting.

He watched in horror as the man tugged on his wife's elbow and pointed at the table. He increased his speed.

Inevitably Ben and the other dad reached the table at the same time.

'It's okay,' he grinned. 'I don't want the table, just the chair.' He swooped it up and began to carry it away before the father who had been already sitting at the table grabbed its leg.

'What do you think you're doing?' he demanded.

'Oh, they've run out of high chairs, so, er, I was just grabbing this one.'

'But we need that high chair,' said the other man who had arrived at the same table at the same time. 'Look, we have a baby with us.' He turned round to point vigorously across the restaurant to his wife, who was struggling to reach them as she was carrying a baby and trying to guide two other children.

'I know but you see we have already sat down so I think we get dibs on this chair,' said Ben, giving it a tug to try and free it from the man's grasp.

He was aware things were coming out of his mouth that were irrational and petty and not in character at all but all he wanted to do was to get the high chair, put Jack in it and get to the all-you-can-eat buffet. Oh, and order a cold beer. Then he would feel like he was really on holiday.

'I think you will both find that we have dibs on the chair,' said the man already at the table. 'We haven't finished yet. We are still to partake of the ice-cream fountain and the chocolate fountain and this high chair isn't going anywhere until I have visited them both, so please get your mitts off our table and our high chair until we have done with them.'

Ben stared at the man who looked tired and frazzled and like he needed a holiday. Like, a proper holiday. Not in a hotel surrounded by a gazillion kids.

'I'm so sorry,' said Ben, putting the chair down gently. 'I don't know what got into me. This place can drive you kind of crazy, can't it?'

The man nodded. 'We go home tomorrow,' he said. Ben knew he was looking forward to it.

'You take the next available chair,' he said to the man standing next to him. 'Jack can sit on my knee. He's older than your baby. He'll cope.'

'Cheers, mate,' nodded the guy back. 'Appreciate that. It's our first day. I hadn't been expecting this.' He cast his hand over the restaurant. Over the chaos and noise.

'Ours too,' said Ben. 'Perhaps you need to come later to eat, do you think?'

'Nine thirty is good,' said the man at the table. 'It's quiet then. Loads of high chairs. We did that one night when Freya couldn't sleep.

Just brought her down in the buggy. Actually that was a good night. Rubbish food left on the buffet, of course, but at least it was quiet.'

'Thanks, mate, see you around,' said Ben, thinking that he couldn't see his lot lasting until nine thirty for food. They'd have to put up with six-thirty chaos all week.

*

'Where's the chair?' asked Katy when he returned to their table.

'They hadn't finished with it,' replied Ben.

'Did they say when they would be finished with it?' demanded Katy.

'No. And I said another family could have it anyway. Their need was greater than ours. We'll cope.'

'Greater than ours?' questioned Katy.

'They had three kids and the guy looked kind of desperate.'

'Oh,' said Katy, looking despondent. 'Everyone is at the buffet so I said I'd stay at the table just in case anyone tried to nick it. Daniel's looking after Millie.'

'Great,' nodded Ben, feeling a bit dazed. 'I'll stay with you and keep you company.'

'Why don't you go and get yourself some food now and then you can come back and then I'll go with Jack and get his food and then he can sit on your knee whilst you both eat,' replied Katy.

Ben stared at her, trying to make sense of what she had just said.

'If you get your food now,' said Katy, 'then at least you will have a head start on eating before I get back with Jack and he has to sit on your knee whilst you both eat. You might at least get a few moments to enjoy your food then.'

Ben nodded but he didn't really understand. Why did eating suddenly require so many logistics? An all-you-can-eat buffet should make life easier for the likes of them surely. Instant food, instant choice. The perfect thing for families. They'd paid quite a lot of extra money for this added convenience and yet the last thing it felt at the moment was convenient. He had *never* had a meal with so many logistical issues.

'Right then,' he said, getting up. 'I'll go grab something, I won't be long.'

*

Actually this was starting to be fun. Ben cruised the food stations picking a bit from here, there and everywhere until his plate looked like a technicoloured food mountain. He was particularly pleased when he found the kids' section and so was able to top his chicken tikka masala with a couple of chicken nuggets and a spoonful of macaroni cheese. Actually, to be honest, he had been a bit dazzled by the array of international foods and, given the logistics he'd so far faced in even getting to the buffet, he was doubtful whether there would be an opportunity for him to approach the laden tables again, so he was keen to pile as much on his plate as possible.

Just as he was about to return to the table, he spotted Daniel standing in line with an empty plate.

'You not eating?' he asked him.

'Yes, maybe next century. I am waiting in line for a freshly cooked omelette by the slowest chef I have ever come across.'

'There's plenty of other stuff to choose from if you don't want to wait,' said Ben.

'No, I think for my first experience in an all-you-can-eat establish-ment I would actually like to see how my food is being cooked and know that it is fresh to my plate and hasn't been mauled over by... by... *other* people. Or, horror of horrors, sat under a lamp.'

Ben looked down at his piled-high plate and shrugged. 'Well, I'm hungry so I'm not going to think about that,' he said cheerfully. 'Good luck.'

Ben returned to the table and welcomed Jack to his knee as Katy got up to go and get some food.

'Good idea getting Jack something to nibble on,' she said, nodding at his plate as Jack reached out and swiped two chicken nuggets from the top of his curry.

'Oi buddy,' Ben said as he watched one of the nuggets disappear into the toddler's mouth. 'Mummy's bringing yours.' Jack looked back at him blankly and picked up the next one.

'Katy!' shouted Ben. She turned back to look at him from half way across the room. 'I think you better bring a bucket of chicken nuggets,' he shouted. He watched, as Katy looked embarrassed before shouting back.

'Okay and I'll bring some more of the carrot sticks that he loves as well.' She turned away quickly, clearly not wanting to hear any more unhealthy requests.

*

Ben didn't think there was actually any one time when all ten of them were sitting at the table. Daniel took forever to sit down as he rejected the first omelette that was made for him at the omelette station, claiming they hadn't cooked the onion enough. Gabriel diligently fed Silvie whilst waiting for Daniel to return but then left him to continue whilst he made his way around the buffet, meaning that Daniel's omelette was cold by the time he got to it and so he joined the back of the omelette queue for the third time in the vague hope that this time he would return to the table and actually be able to eat his meal. It was looking likely that Daniel would be banned from the omelette station by breakfast the next day.

Logan wasn't too happy with his high chair and was determined to make a break for it, causing Braindead to rush through his pile of food at indigestion speed so he could set him free. When Logan was eventually allowed out of the chair he wandered around all the tables escorted by a very patient Braindead, who managed to occasionally veer him close to the bread table so he could grab a roll to munch on.

Abby picked at her food, bringing small portions back to the table, pushing it around with her fork and then shoving the plate forward to indicate she was done and it could be cleared away. She would then sigh and get up and repeat the whole process again until she discovered the ice-cream fountain and brought a huge pile of Mister Softee back to her place and proceeded to devour it.

'Everybody freeze,' said Braindead as he approached the table, looking longingly at the plate full of cakes and ice cream that Ben had managed to entice Jack back to the buffet with. 'Photo op, I reckon.' He pulled his phone out of his back pocket whilst holding onto Logan with his other hand. 'You take Logan,' he said to Abby, 'and I'll try and take a picture.'

'I'll take it,' she said, leaping up and pulling her phone out. 'You get in the picture.'

'But don't you want to be in the picture?' asked Braindead.

'Not really,' she said bluntly. 'Go on, you sit down.'

Braindead shuffled back into his seat and hauled Logan onto his knee. 'Everyone say "happy holidays"!' he exclaimed, a massive grin on his face.

Nobody spoke.

'Everyone say "cheese",' he said.

'Cheese,' came the muffled reply as Abby clicked away.

'Now you get in the picture,' said Braindead, leaping up and handing Logan to Abby. 'Come on, you need to be in one as well.'

'No, really,' she said. 'I'm not bothered.'

'Come on, Abby, please. First holiday with Logan and all that. Come on, we need a picture of the two of you together.'

Abby just looked at him for a moment and said nothing until she eventually slumped down in the seat.

'Now, "cheese" everyone again,' said Braindead.

'We've lost Millie,' announced Katy. 'She's gone to get more ice cream.'

'Ah well, she was in the first one.'

'Ice cream, Mummy,' said Logan, looking up at Abby.

'See, he wants ice cream,' said Abby, getting up and handing Logan back to his dad. 'You'd better take him.'

'Right,' said Braindead. 'Right. We've got plenty of time for photos this week, haven't we? Let's take some on the beach tomorrow.'

'I'm not going on the beach tomorrow,' said Abby.

'Why not?' replied Braindead.

'I might get burnt before we go out at night. I might just stay in the room all day.'

'Ice cream, Daddy,' interrupted Logan.

'Sure thing,' Braindead said, turning his back on his wife.

Chapter Eleven

Katy had no idea what to wear to a hen night out in Spain with a group of girls she'd only met for a couple of hours on the plane. It was insane. Quite apart from the fact she hadn't packed for a hen party. She'd packed for a family holiday so her clothes consisted of swimsuits with hidden magic panels that kept your belly in and cover-up kaftans for hiding cellulite on the beach and maxi dresses in case she didn't have time to shave her legs. She also had a full plethora of comfortable shoes. Painful feet became extremely unnecessary, Katy had found, the minute you became a mother.

The day had passed by fairly uneventfully. Apart from the ridiculously early start, of course. Jack had woken up at 5.30 a.m. so Ben had put him in the bed between them but of course he'd wriggled and squirmed, making sleep completely impossible. Still, at least it meant they had been ridiculously early for breakfast, so had their pick of the tables and of the high chairs.

Katy couldn't help but yawn as she surveyed the wardrobe and plucked out a knee-length cotton dress, which would have to do, and some sparkly flip-flops. They were comfortable, functional and most definitely shouted, *I am a mother and wife and absolutely not interested in being harassed by lecherous men even if I am out on a hen do.*

She managed to find some shimmering eyeshadow and some fairly vivid lip-gloss, which did lift her appearance, and then contemplated whether a black leather bumbag would be acceptable. Maybe not. It was possible Daniel would never speak to her again if she made him go out with her wearing a bumbag.

She glanced at her phone. Yet another message appeared on the screen from Cassie. To say that Katy had received a positive response from her when she had texted to say they were coming out was an understatement. Cassie had clearly been through the whole emoji catalogue to convey how grateful/happy/ecstatic/delighted/over the moon she was and had sent Katy further texts throughout the day to check she was still coming. It was nice to be so wanted but Katy couldn't help thinking that there was something very wrong when the most important person attending your hen party was a complete stranger you'd met on the plane on the way there. She put her phone in her bag and took one last look at her reflection. 'Middle-aged' was the only word that sprang to mind but it would have to do.

When Katy arrived in reception, Daniel was already there in a pristine pastel pink linen shirt looking very suitable for one of those upmarket hen dos where champagne was quaffed and funny stories about the bride-to-be were shared over canapés. Katy very much doubted that this night out would be anything like that. There was an air of calm as the kids sat plugged into headphones and iPads. Silvie was in her pushchair being quietly rocked by Gabriel with a towel draped over the hood. Presumably she was fast asleep. Everyone else was sipping on bottles of ice-cold beer, including Ollie, who looked very comfortable sitting between Ben and Braindead. They had seen him by the pool earlier and he'd been invited to the boys' babysitting session this evening, which he had gratefully accepted, stating that he couldn't bear to spend another night in the honeymoon suite, brushing up rose petals.

'You look nice,' said Ben to Katy.

'You not changed yet?' asked Daniel.

'Thank you, husband,' she replied to Ben. 'Get stuffed, ex best friend,' she told Daniel.

She plonked herself down on a spare seat. 'No Abby yet?' she asked Braindead.

He shook his head but said nothing else, instead staring at the TV screen showing some random football match over the bar.

'Can't remember the last hen do I went on,' she said to no-one in particular. 'Years ago, I reckon, can't even really remember what you're supposed to do.'

'I had a stag do,' muttered Ollie, taking a large swig of his drink.

'Seriously!' replied Braindead, suddenly alert.

'Oh yeah, she let me do that. Had a cracking weekend in Wales actually. You know, at one of those outward bound places. Really enjoyed it.'

'So all was not lost then,' said Braindead. 'You got a good weekend away with your mates even if you didn't get married.'

'Guess so,' shrugged Ollie. 'They made me get a tattoo though,' he added. 'I didn't want one but we were playing this stupid game and somehow I lost and I had to have a tattoo. The good thing was I got to choose where and what.'

'So let's see it then,' said Daniel, leaning over. 'Did you make sure you got something cool like a Chinese proverb or something?'

'You really don't want to see it,' sighed Ollie.

'Go on, don't be shy,' said Daniel. 'I always think it shows so much about someone's personality when it comes to what you have tattooed about your person. It's an insight into their soul, I think.'

'I really don't think you want to see it,' repeated Ollie.

'Aw, mate, come on,' said Ben. 'Or would you prefer to show us tomorrow night on the lads' night out?' he added.

'No way!' shrieked Daniel. 'I want to see it. Come on, Ollie, just show us.'

Ollie downed the rest of his drink before standing up and turning around. He unbuttoned his fly and then pulled down the back of his shorts to reveal the top of his left buttock and the horror story tattooed on it.

'Oh my God,' gasped Katy. 'Oh my God, that is a disaster. What on earth made you do that?' she asked.

'I thought it was a good idea at the time,' replied Ollie, peering over his shoulder to try and take a look at his massive mistake.

'Perhaps you could tattoo something else over it,' said Daniel, screwing his face up, clearly not impressed.

Braindead was just laughing, heaving his shoulders up and down.

'That's not very kind,' Katy told him. 'He wasn't to know, was he?'

'Epic fail, lad,' said Braindead, wiping the tears away from his eyes. 'Really, could it be any worse? You are a walking disaster.'

Gabriel heard the commotion and peered round to see what everyone else was looking at.

'Who is Ellie?' he asked on reading the name beautifully etched on Ollie's backside and encased in an elegant red heart with Cupid's arrow pierced through it.

Everyone else stifled their laughter whilst Gabriel looked around him, confused. Then a look of realisation crossed his face.

'Is she your ex fiancée?' he asked. 'Why did you do that?'

'Because I thought she was going to marry me!' said Ollie, doing up his trousers and sitting down again red-faced. 'Surely it's a pretty safe bet to get your fiancé's name tattooed on your backside a couple of months before you get married?'

'You really had no idea then?' said Katy.

'No,' said Ollie, picking his drink up and looking as if he didn't want to talk about it any more.

'I'll design something to cover it up,' offered Daniel. 'Something you'll be proud of. It's what I do,' he added. 'Let me take a picture and I'll come up with something that will make sense.' He reached inside his trouser pocket for his phone.

'I'm not getting it out again,' said Ollie grimly, staring up at the TV screen, making it clear that the subject was closed.

'Well, let me know if you change your mind,' Daniel replied, putting his phone away again. 'Anytime.'

Katy watched as the arrival of someone momentarily distracted two men at the bar. She saw one nudge the other and indicate towards the door. Katy turned to look at what had captured their attention only to find Abby strutting towards them in the most spectacularly tight dress, displaying the most spectacular cleavage. She looked sensational. Katy gulped. Her cotton dress and sparkly flip-flops would look horrifically dowdy next to the sexpot walking towards them.

Katy turned to look at Braindead, who had seen his wife enter the room but had a very blank expression on his face like he wasn't really seeing her. Sure, Abby had always been a glamour puss but this was a grade above even by her standards. This was *Love Island* level that took your breath away. Skin-tight clothing, towering heels and immaculate, if abundant, make-up. Her naturally wavy blonde hair had also been ironed perfectly straight, giving her that sleek sexy look that you rarely saw on the mother of a fifteen-month-old.

'Who is that?' Katy heard Ollie mutter. 'She's new.'

'That's my wife,' said Braindead, standing up. 'You look great,' he told her, taking a step forward and kissing her cheek.

'Do you think?' she said, suddenly looking a bit nervous.

'Definitely,' he nodded before the match on the screen distracted him. 'Do you have enough cash with you, and is your phone fully charged?' he asked her, still looking at the screen.

'Yes,' said Abby. 'Of course. I have been out on the town before, you know.'

'Sure,' said Braindead, sitting down, still unable to drag his eyes away from the football.

Everyone hovered. Katy glanced at Ben, who pulled a face.

'So shall we go then?' said Abby, turning her back on everyone.

'Yes,' said Daniel, getting up and straightening his trousers. 'Let's, shall we?' He held his arm up for Abby, who took it whilst smoothing down her hair for the trillionth time. 'Don't worry, guys,' he said over his shoulder to Ben and Braindead. 'I'll look after these two vixens and I'll be sure to have them home by midnight.'

'Midnight!' chimed Katy and Abby.

'There's no way I can stay out until midnight,' said Katy, already feeling like this was going to be the longest night ever.

'There's no way I'm coming back before midnight,' said Abby. 'Nowhere gets going round here before midnight. It's going to be late,' she told Braindead. 'I'll see you when I see you.'

'Right,' said Braindead. He grabbed Katy's arm just as she was about to head away. 'Look after her,' he said. 'Won't you?'

'I'll try,' she replied.

He nodded and turned back to the football.

Chapter Twelve

The three of them didn't say much as they walked out of the hotel and into the fading sunlight. Katy felt apprehensive. What with Braindead's words ringing in her ears, and Abby's look of utter determination on her face, Katy didn't think she had any power whatsoever to influence how the night might turn out.

'Not sure what to expect, are you?' said Katy in an effort to make conversation.

'Trashy and tarty,' said Daniel, 'that's what I reckon.'

'Great,' groaned Katy.

'But good trashy and tarty,' added Daniel. 'Unapologetic, honest, authentic trashy and tarty.'

'Is that a thing?' asked Katy.

'Of course it's a thing,' said Daniel. 'There are fashionistas the world over trying to recreate the trash/tart look but it's false, it's dishonest, it lacks truth. These fashion bloggers just need to follow a hen do in Spain and then they'll get it. They'll get that trashy and tarty belongs in the British bars of the Mediterranean and not in the likes of Hoxton and Shoreditch.'

'Have you been saving that speech for this moment?' asked Katy.

'I have to admit that I was mulling it over in bed last night whilst Gabriel settled Silvie. I might post it online when I get home. Put a little Instagram post together. I could take some pictures tonight, how good would that be? We could do a little vlog about it. Compare the fashions of the Irish bar vis-à-vis the English bar, see if we can discover any discernible differences that might be of interest to the great fashion-buying public.'

'You do talk utter bullshit sometimes,' muttered Katy.

'How about you, Abby? Fancy starring in my vlog? You'd make a great frontman for the mini documentary that will be called "Two Women and a Gay Man Go on a Stranger's Hen Night". Got a ring to it, don't you think? Sounds intriguing, interesting, mysterious. Why are they going on a stranger's hen night? What will happen, will they all come out alive?'

Abby wasn't answering, just looking far off into the distance. Katy and Daniel exchanged looks.

'Right, let's have a picture,' declared Daniel, leaping out in front of them and whipping his phone out. 'Before and after, hey?'

They stood in a line whilst Daniel stretched his arm out in front of them in order to fit in their grinning heads.

'Say "chocolate penis",' he declared. 'I tell you what, I was *made* to go on a hen night. I've got all the right phrases.'

He put his phone away and they carried on walking past the already filling up bars and restaurants. Everyone looked lively, way too lively, whereas Katy felt anything but.

'I don't know about you guys,' she said, 'but I'm all up for sloping off at a sensible hour. I'm sure Cassie won't miss us if we bail early. It's not like she really knows us, is it? Can't quite believe she's so keen for us to be there in the first place, to be honest.'

'I'm staying out,' said Abby. 'I'm staying out until the end.'

'Right, okay,' said Katy.

'You don't have to stay though,' said Abby, turning to look at her. 'I'll be fine. You go home whenever you want.'

*

The participants on the hen night were well away by the time Katy, Daniel and Abby found the bar they were meeting in.

Abby, who had been reserved and quiet during their ten-minute walk, approached the group like long-lost friends, throwing her arms in the air and hugging each and every one of them whilst Katy looked on awkwardly.

Katy was also horrified to see that they were all in co-ordinated outfits. Each one was wearing some kind of eighties neon nightmare in the form of leotards or leggings and leg warmers and, worst of all, towelling headbands. Even their drinks were co-ordinated as they all sipped on huge glasses of bright green cocktails.

'I didn't realise there was a dress code,' said Daniel, throwing his arms in the air, waving in distress at his linen outfit.

'You're here!' cried Cassie, dashing up to them. 'You're here,' she said again, engulfing Katy in her arms. 'I'm so glad you are here.'

'Well, we were delighted to be invited,' said Katy politely, thinking that at this very moment she would rather be anywhere else other than spending the evening with this much Lycra.

'You don't have to do anything Ruth tells you to,' Cassie told her urgently. 'Honestly. Just say no. But you'll need to be firm.'

Ruth walked over to them in an ill-fitting pink leotard, black leggings, green leg warmers and a big blonde wig.

'Don't worry,' she said as she approached. 'We bought you some accessories to make sure you didn't feel left out.' She delved in a bag and dragged out three neon towelling headbands and three pairs of neon mesh gloves. Daniel looked at them in horror.

'It's an eighties theme,' Ruth told him.

'Oh I get that,' he replied. 'But why?'

'Because on the hour every hour we shall be performing an aerobics routine to "Let's Get Physical" by Olivia Newton-John. No matter where we are or what we are doing, we must be together and we must do the routine. Now you have a pass out of the first one seeing as it's very nearly eight o'clock. You can watch how it's done and then Rachel has agreed that she will take you round the back and teach it to you.'

Daniel and Katy stared at her, gobsmacked. Then they stared at each other and then back at Ruth.

'No, I don't think—' began Katy.

'There's always a theme, you see,' interrupted Ruth, 'and there always has to be a dance. Last year for Marnie's we came as ringmasters with canes and did *The Greatest Showman*. You should have seen the crowd that gathered at two in the morning outside McDonald's in Tenerife and filmed us. We even got on YouTube. Can you believe it? Hopefully someone will spot us this time and put us on again. We could become YouTube sensations.' Ruth grinned at them as she grabbed her drink and took a massive slurp.

Katy could feel Daniel shuddering. He looked down at the towelling ring in his hands and she thought he might cry.

Ruth glanced at her watch and, to the horror of both Katy and Daniel, took a whistle out of the neon yellow bumbag attached to her waist. She poised the whistle at her lips as she stared down at her watch. They could see her nodding the seconds down until she looked up and blew hard. Everyone in the group downed their drinks, slapped the glasses on the tables and made their way to a clearing at the front of the bar, where the inhabitants and also those passing by could see them.

Ruth reached down behind her and lifted a huge ghetto blaster up, handing it to Daniel.

'Would you press play on my signal?' she said.

Daniel nodded numbly, clearly not quite believing what he was seeing.

Ruth walked over to the group and stood in front of them with her arm raised. They shuffled into two lines, some of them shaking out limbs as if warming up. Cassie was at the back, trying to hide behind everyone else.

Ruth blew her whistle again and nodded at Daniel, who glanced at Katy, horrified, before cautiously pressing down on the play button.

The eighties track filled the air as Olivia Neutron-Bomb's voice emerged. In front of them the group started to sway and then went into a full-on Grapevine followed by star jumps, which certainly caught the attention of the assembled male drinkers.

'Oh my God,' muttered Daniel, clutching at Katy's arm. 'Is this really happening or am I having some weird retro dream? I've kind of always had a thing about Olivia Newton-John. That's why I'm seeing this, isn't it?' he said to her, a desperate look in his eyes. 'I'm seeing this because I have a deep-down fetish for Olivia and it's resurfacing now in my worst possible nightmare.'

'You had a thing for Olivia Newton-John?' she asked him, astonished.

'Oh yeah,' replied Daniel. 'Who wouldn't? All those headbands and hair ribbons and then the leather skin-tight catsuit. I mean, seriously?'

Katy looked back to where the hen party were doing burpees, some of them starting to sweat in the heat and the Lycra.

'I'm sorry to tell you that this is real,' said Katy, putting her hands on his shoulders. 'You are standing in a bar in Spain about to embark on a night out with a bunch of women who on the hour every hour will be telling you to don a fluorescent yellow headband and perform a choreographed fitness routine to "Let's Get Physical" for all the world to see.'

'You know there is only one way of dealing with this, don't you?' said Daniel.

'Agreed,' replied Katy.

'Should we start with shots?' he asked.

'Several,' said Katy, glancing at her watch. 'We only have an hour to numb the pain.'

*

It was after ten o clock before they sat down to eat. Katy had been treading the very thin line of being drunk enough on an empty stomach for the hourly dance performance but sober enough to maintain some degree of control. Despite Cassie's promise, saying no to Ruth had proved to be impossible. During their first performance, she had physically dragged Katy and Daniel to the front of the line-up and held their hands in a vice-like grip until the torture was over. Cassie had looked on apologetically but powerlessly. It was possibly the hardest night out Katy had ever been on. She was alternating between sipping drinks and then downing them faster than lemonade as each performance loomed. She hoped that now they were sitting down to eat that perhaps they would be here for at least an hour and that the eleven o'clock showing would be forgotten.

It was utter chaos trying to order. Eventually the waiter stood on a chair and shouted at them all to shut up, which they did until he began to repeat back their choices and then they heckled him until he threw his hands in the air and stood down. Katy watched as Daniel put his hand on the poor lad's arm and told him just to bring what he thought they had ordered and put it in the middle of the table. No-one cared what they were eating, they were only interested in the jugs of sangria that were a bit too slow in appearing.

After the waiter scampered off, Ruth took his position on the chair and blew her whistle. The whole table went quiet.

'Now let's have a bit of hush here, shall we?' she said. 'Time for some serious business. So, we all know why we are here,' she began.

'To get pissed and feel men's arses,' one woman piped up.

'Down you,' shouted Ruth back. 'Down you, or else I will be ringing your husband.'

'Oh, the bastard will be fiddling with his bits and pieces somewhere, he won't care about me feeling some arses this weekend.'

Daniel raised his eyebrows at Katy.

'Now, now, we need to be setting a good example, don't we, which is exactly what we are going to do next. I'm handing round some pieces of paper and pens and I want you all to write down your best piece of advice for Cassie as she embarks on married life.'

'Don't do it,' someone piped up. 'I wish someone had said that to me before I'd got married.'

'Shut up,' said Ruth. 'For those of you who *are* already married, you also need to write down what the best thing about getting married is. Got it? Now I'm going to blow my whistle and then you will have two minutes to write everything down and then we will read them out. So, on your marks, get set, go.'

She blew her whistle and sat herself back down at the table.

'She's a hen party Nazi,' Daniel whispered in Katy's ear. 'We need to execute a great escape. I'm not enjoying this.'

'Well, Abby certainly is,' said Katy, nodding to where Abby was sitting opposite them, nestled between two girls who had taken her under their wing. They had included her on their first round of Jäger-bombs and after that it had been as though they had been separated at birth as they'd giggled their way round the bars of Spain. Katy had stalked Abby into the toilets earlier just to get her alone and to see if she was okay and been dismissed with an 'Why on earth would I not be okay? I'm having the time of my life.' Then she had stumbled out of the bathroom and not talked to her since.

'Can't we leave her?' said Daniel. 'She's a big girl.'

Katy looked over to where Abby and her new mates were downing half pints of sangria.

'I'm not sure,' she said. 'Let's see how things stand after the meal.'

Katy glanced over at Cassie, who had been put at the head of the table by Ruth. She looked resigned and had by no means clamoured to be centre of all the attention. In fact, most of the time she was doing her best to fade into the background.

The whistle sounded out loud and clear yet again, causing Katy to jump. She was really sick of that whistle. She might have to steal it and wrap it around Ruth's neck.

'So who's going to start then?' Ruth asked. 'Shall we begin with you, Bridget?' she said to the girl right beside her.

Bridget frowned and picked up her piece of paper.

'I'm not married,' she announced.

'Because you are scary as hell and every bloke I know is scared shitless of you,' shouted out another girl.

'Fuck off,' said Bridget, standing up and pointing a neon mesh-covered finger at her.

'It's true,' the other girl replied. 'My Tony said you eat balls for breakfast.'

'I'd eat his if he had any,' declared Bridget.

'You leave my Tony alone,' said the other girl, standing up.

'Now, now, girls,' said Daniel, standing up too and raising his hands. 'Tonight is all about Cassie and not Tony's balls so shall we get back to what we're here for? Would you both like to sit down?'

Both women looked at him in awe then meekly sat down.

'Continue, Bridget,' said Daniel, taking his seat again.

'Well done,' whispered Katy.

'A gay man can diffuse a bitch fight quicker than a dose of salt can evaporate a slug. Did you know that?' he said, turning towards her. 'You put salt on a slug and it just dissolves, just like that.'

Katy stared at him as she heard them being shushed by the gathering around them.

Bridget cleared her throat and looked at Cassie.

'My advice to you is be yourself,' she said before swallowing hard. 'Stay being Cassie. Don't change.'

She sat down abruptly to near silence.

Daniel stood up and gave her a massive round of applause.

'Excellent work,' he declared. 'Excellent.'

'That's good,' agreed Ruth. 'Now next we have Heather.'

Heather stood up and giggled, casting her eyes around the table.

'Just remember,' she said. 'Marriage isn't perfect…' She paused, as there was much muttering about the table from those who were married. 'It's just two imperfect people who refuse to give up on each other.'

'Oh my God, Heather,' exclaimed one of the women sitting next to Abby. 'That is the cheesiest thing I have ever heard.'

Heather went bright red. 'I… I…' she spluttered. 'I got it off a website on advice about marriage. I thought it was kind of cute.' She sat down with a thump.

Daniel stood up again and gave her a round of applause. 'Do you know what, I like that,' he said. 'It's so true. You may think to look at me that I'm perfect but I do have my faults and my husband deals with them with style and finesse. I think it's cute too, very cute.'

Next came one of Abby's new best friends, Fi. She burst into laughter several times before she managed to splutter any words out, as though she were back at school and afraid of being seen to try too hard.

'My advice is,' she said eventually. 'To think of Ryan Gosling whenever you need to, you know…' She collapsed into giggles again, falling back in her chair.

'Ryan fucking Gosling?' said Bridget. 'Can't you do better than that?'

'My thoughts entirely,' agreed Daniel. 'But Ryan Reynolds? Now you're talking.'

'Oh my God, yes,' declared Bridget. 'Especially in *Deadpool*. Especially in that outfit.'

She looked genuinely excited.

'Which one is Ryan Reynolds?' whispered Katy to Daniel.

'Have you not seen *Deadpool*?' he asked her.

She shook her head.

'You frighten me sometimes,' he replied. 'Let's see. Do you remember the film with Sandra Bullock called *The Proposal*?'

'Was he the guy in that?' she asked. 'The guy who was married to Scarlett Johansson and then married Blake Lively?'

'Yes,' nodded Daniel. 'Of course I might have known that you would be able to identify him through his private life rather than his cinematic achievements. I so need to ban you from the *Daily Mail* website.'

'He's hot,' she agreed. 'Is he hot in *Deadpool* then?'

'He wears a scuzzy red and black rubber suit.'

'Okay, not his best look then?'

'Most certainly not but clearly Bridget thinks differently.'

'Right, who's next?' said Ruth, getting them all to quieten down again. 'Are you ready, Abby?' she asked.

Abby stared at her for a moment.

'You're amongst friends,' said Ruth. 'You're part of our gang now.'

Abby slowly stood up and took out her piece of paper. She looked down and swallowed then cleared her throat. She glanced over at Cassie. Katy found herself holding her breath.

'Getting married was the best day of my life,' she said. Katy let out her breath. 'Enjoy the day because it will pass so fast,' she continued. 'The best thing about being married is… is… the great party you have when you are the centre of attention, the centre of his attention, and you know at that moment you are the most important person on the planet and that is the best feeling.' She closed her eyes for a moment. 'My advice is to make the most of that feeling.'

She sat down with a thump and immediately grabbed her glass and downed her drink. Daniel leapt up and started to fist-pump the air.

'Yeah, Abby,' he said. 'You go, girl. You go.'

Everyone else politely clapped as Daniel sat down.

'You are a regular cheerleader tonight,' said Katy.

'Well, someone had to lift that out of the gutter, didn't they? What's going on with that girl?'

Katy shrugged. 'Whatever it is, it isn't good. That was way deep. Way too deep for Abby.'

'Mmmm,' agreed Daniel. 'Abby doesn't normally do deep, does she?'

'And next it's Rachel,' announced Ruth. 'Come on, girl, up you get.'

Rachel rose up giggling and steadied herself against the table as she squinted at her piece of paper.

'Not brought my glasses out,' she muttered. 'And I can't remember what I wrote.'

'You idiot,' said Fi, grabbing at the paper. She held it to her face, trying to make out what was written. 'How drunk are you?' she asked. 'I can't read a word of it.'

'Give it back,' protested Rachel, trying to grab it but proceeding to rip the piece of paper in half.

'Bloody shambles,' muttered Daniel under his breath.

'Just tell us what you wrote,' said Ruth, checking her watch.

'Well, erm, I think I wrote that she should never ever clean the toilet because, once you do, that's it, your husband will just think that the cleaning fairies clean the toilet and so will never bother to clean up after himself.'

'Do you know what?' said Katy to Daniel. 'I think that is the best advice so far. Seriously.'

'And the best thing about being married is that you don't have to try any more really, do you? If you want to eat a whole packet of doughnuts you can, or go down the shop in your slippers it doesn't matter, or if you go out with no make-up, it's all good. Like, he doesn't care and he can't care because he married you, right, in sickness and in health till death do us part, so it means you can do what you like. How immense is that? When I married Jacob it was like a weight had been lifted off my shoulders. Literally. I didn't even have to hide the fact any more that I watch *Corrie* and *EastEnders* every night. I just watch it and he puts up with it. It's brilliant being married, honestly, Cassie. You are going to love it!'

'You got married so you didn't have to hide your soap opera addiction?' questioned Daniel.

'No!' protested Rachel. 'I'm just saying it's one of the hidden benefits not many people talk about. You know that actually being married gives you a lot of freedom, I reckon.'

She sat down.

'Daniel?' said Ruth.

'Yes?' replied Daniel, still staring at Rachel.

'Would you like to add any pearls of wisdom?'

'Oh, yes, of course. Yes, certainly I would.' He stood up and straightened his collar. He didn't pick up his sheet of paper. Katy knew Daniel well – he would have memorised it for maximum impact.

'Cassie, darling,' he said. 'I don't know you well as we only met on the plane, what, two days ago and I am so honoured to be part of this special occasion…'

Katy put her head in her hands. Why did he always have to make it all about him?

'I got married just under two years ago to my amazing husband Gabriel. We actually had two weddings. We had a not-really-a-wedding wedding in a circus tent, where I told him my love was the size of an elephant, and then we actually got married right here in Spain because Gabriel is Spanish and we came to get married here because his father was marrying Katy's mother and so—'

'So are you brother and sister?' asked Bridget.

'Good God no!' exclaimed Daniel. 'We're not related. Only through marriage. My father-in-law is married to Katy's mother.'

'Right,' nodded Bridget. No-one spoke as they tried to work that one out.

'Anyway, as I was saying, we had two weddings but that is by the by because you asked for advice on getting married and all I would say is this… and I'd actually like to quote Abby's husband over there, who made the most moving speech at our not-really-a-wedding. What he said was, and correct me if I am wrong, Abby, but he said, "Love is easy, it's life that's hard,' and what he meant was that as long as you have love you will be fine because that will keep you going through the difficult bits – because you *will* have difficult bits, Cassie. When Gabriel and I first moved in together it took me some time to make him understand that he didn't have to do the washing, for example. Now that could have really come between us but we talked it through and we had a hug and now he knows that the cleaner does the washing, but you see, we knew we could get past it because we had love to keep us together. Does that make sense?'

It was the quietest the table had been all evening.

'You have a cleaner?' asked Bridget in awe.

'Of course,' said Daniel.

'I've never met anyone who has cleaner before,' she said. 'I know loads of people who are cleaners but never met someone who actually has one. Are you, like, really posh or something?'

Daniel surveyed Bridget as Katy surveyed Daniel. How on earth was he going to answer that question? She knew that Daniel liked to consider himself as very posh indeed really but she also knew that he was aware that perhaps it wasn't something to show off about right now.

'No,' he said eventually. 'I like to think of myself as classless. I've worked hard to get where I am and get myself into a position where I can employ a cleaner and I'm proud of that. I don't think that makes me posh.'

'I'd like to earn enough money to have a cleaner,' said Bridget.

'You work hard and it might happen one day,' said Daniel whilst Katy squirmed.

Bridget nodded at him earnestly.

Ruth suddenly blasted on her whistle, making everyone jump.

'Well, I think that's enough from Daniel,' she said. 'Now what about you, Katy?'

Katy stared up at her like a rabbit in the headlights. Her mind had gone a complete blank the minute that Ruth had laid down the challenge, only capable of bland, pathetic advice unlikely to be useful. Everyone was distracted for a moment as Abby and Fi burst into peals of giggles then refused to share the joke. Katy took a deep breath and stood up.

'I would like to thank you first, Cassie, for inviting us. It's really very kind of you.' She heard Daniel humph behind her. 'And then what I want to say is that... that...' she glanced over at Abby again. 'That the key is communication, just talk to each other, whatever you are thinking or feeling, you have to communicate. I can't tell you how important that is, Abby.'

'Cassie, you mean,' urged Daniel, tugging on her arm.

'What?' said Katy, looking at him in surprise.

'You said Abby,' he said. 'You mean Cassie, right?'

'Did I?'

'Yes,' he nodded.

Christ, thought Katy. She needed to get a grip. 'Sorry,' she spluttered. 'This sangria must be really good,' she giggled, holding up her glass. 'Shall we have a toast to... to... communication?'

Daniel shook his head in despair but nonetheless stood up and raised his glass gallantly.

'Communication,' he said as everyone murmured after him.

Katy sat down feeling mortified and took another slug of her drink, wishing the ground would swallow her up.

'And what is the best thing about being married then, Katy?' asked Ruth.

Oh God, thought Katy, when would this ever end?

'Right, yes, of course,' she said, trying to gather herself. She glanced over at Abby, who was giving her a weird look. 'The best thing about being married actually is having someone to share everything with, especially the babies you make.' Inexplicably she felt the tears spring to her eyes as an image of Millie and Jack fighting on the bed came to her. 'Knowing you made them together and they are totally yours and you will share them for the rest of your lives, well, it's by far the most magical thing about being married.'

Katy had reduced everyone around the room to silence yet again.

'Not that you have to have children to be happily married of course,' she added, suddenly panicking that maybe there were women around the table who were married and had either decided not to have kids or couldn't have them. She quickly scanned the table for signs of distress. Everyone appeared to have switched off and was either chatting amongst themselves or looking into space. Apart from Daniel, who was glaring at her.

'And of course...' she said, clutching his arm. 'You know if you can't actually physically have a baby because you, erm... haven't got the necessary equipment...' she trailed off.

'Like a womb,' said Daniel.

'Yes,' she nodded. 'I guess that's what I meant. If you don't have a womb between you then that's okay too. Sharing the upbringing of a child, any child, is the most bonding experience you could ask for.'

'Do you have a kid?' Bridget demanded of Daniel.

'Yes, we do,' replied Daniel proudly.

'You and your husband?' she asked.

'Yes, that's right. Her name is Silvie and she is nine months old.'

'How come?' asked Bridget.

'Do you mean how come we have a baby?' replied Daniel.

She nodded.

'We used a surrogate,' he replied.

Bridget stared at him for a moment.

'Do you have to have sex with the surrogate and how did you choose who would have to have sex with a woman?'

Daniel laughed. 'No, we didn't have to do any of that. We used artificial insemination. So my husband and I donated sperm.'

'So whose sperm made the baby?' asked Bridget.

Daniel looked startled for a moment before he replied. 'We don't know,' he said. 'We deliberately left it to chance.'

'Oh,' said Bridget, clearly mulling this revelation over. 'But you must have an idea,' she continued. 'Does she look more like one of you?'

Daniel stared back at her, looking very uncomfortable. He clearly wasn't enjoying this line of questioning.

'No, she doesn't,' he said firmly before turning to Ruth. 'I believe it's your turn,' he said.

'Well, er, I... well, I don't normally take part in these things,' she said. 'I just run them, because someone has to. I mean, it would all fall apart if I didn't run them.'

'Rubbish,' said Daniel. 'You've had just as much time to gather your thoughts on the matter as everyone else and I assume that as you have been on so many hen nights that your views on marriage must be very interesting.'

Ruth looked dumbfounded.

'Well, er, I think that my advice would be that... that...' She started shaking her head as if she couldn't go on but then she suddenly sniffed and gathered herself. 'Enjoy this bit. Enjoy this week, enjoy your wedding day. It's the best time of your life. Seriously. And then... and then just don't forget your mates, hey? You'll still need them after you're married. If not more.' She looked down and swallowed then looked up again with a slightly watery smile.

Then Ruth blew her whistle again and Katy glanced with horror at her watch: it was eleven o'clock on the dot. The ghetto blaster appeared on the table and spontaneously everyone rose from their seats and staggered towards the back corner of the restaurant.

Katy sighed and put on her neon headband.

Chapter Thirteen

'I suppose we'd better go to bed,' announced Ben suddenly, stirring in his chair in the hotel bar. He must have fallen asleep. He started checking around him for Jack and Millie. Jack was fast asleep in his pushchair and Millie was sitting next to him still plugged into the iPad watching *Cinderella*. He glanced at his watch: it was nearly eleven o'clock.

'Jesus,' he said, rubbing his eyes. 'We *really* need to go to bed.' Katy had warned him about not going to bed too late, as she feared that would put the kids in a bad mood all day tomorrow. This could prove catastrophic.

He nudged Braindead who was sitting on a sofa opposite him, his head lolling back, gently snoring, Logan curled up asleep on his lap.

'Oi,' he shouted. 'We need to go to bed.'

'What!' said Braindead, flinging his eyes open in confusion. 'Are they back?'

'No, who knows when they'll be back,' said Ben. 'But we really should take these kids to bed and act like the responsible fathers that we are.'

Braindead clutched his son to his chest. 'He's going to play football for Norway, you know,' he announced suddenly.

'Who is?'

'Logan.'

'How come?'

'I just dreamt it,' said Braindead. 'And you will never guess what, but my great granddad was Norwegian and Norway always have a shit football team so it could happen, couldn't it? Perhaps I should look into getting him a Norwegian passport and then, even if he can half-kick a ball, he should get in the national team. Good, eh? My son playing football for his country. I really couldn't be prouder.'

Ben was too tired to unpick Braindead's logic.

'Where are Ollie and Gabriel?' asked Braindead.

'Oh, they went to change bedrooms and I've not seen them since. They must have crashed.'

Earlier in the evening Ollie had confessed that he was avoiding going to bed as he hated going back to the honeymoon suite on his own and please would someone take it off his hands. Braindead had suggested that they solve it by having a table football tournament, which Ben and Gabriel had agreed seemed like an excellent way to decide who should get the prized room.

It turned out that Gabriel was a crack hand at table football and trounced them both, for which he had apologised profusely. To be fair, both Ben and Braindead had been hampered by the inclusion of their children in the game. Millie had insisted on playing goalie for her dad but couldn't get her timing right and so inevitably would begin spinning her man way after the ball had fallen into the hole behind him, much to Ben's distress.

'No!' he'd cried the first time it happened. 'Like this, Millie.'

'But I did do it like that,' she said.

'But you have to do it quicker,' responded Ben. 'Shall I do the goalie and you do mid-field?'

'But I want to be goalie,' she insisted.

'But you're not very good at it. We're losing,' he replied.

To which she stuck her bottom lip out. It trembled so alarmingly that Ben was forced to tell her that she was learning very fast and should just keep trying.

Braindead didn't fare any better with his son, who demanded having a go at all the handles whenever Braindead let go of one and developed an impressive skill of scoring home goals.

'Goal!!' shouted Logan at one point.

'Wrong goal,' shouted Braindead back, trying very hard to suppress his frustration.

'Perhaps Logan could help me,' said Gabriel at one point. 'To make it fair.'

But Braindead and Ben had agreed that Gabriel would probably trounce them anyway and so he truly deserved to sleep in the honeymoon suite. Gabriel then suggested that they all take it in turns to have the room like the true gentlemen he was, which Ben and Braindead had agreed to happily.

'Did you see that goal he got in against you? It was outstanding,' observed Braindead.

'He confessed later on that he used to play every day when he was growing up in his dad's bar.'

'Seriously!' exclaimed Braindead. 'Well, that explains it then. At least we all get a go. Looking forward to taking Logan for his first hot tub.'

'Right,' said Ben. 'Not Abby then?'

'What?' replied Braindead. 'Oh yeah. I guess she'll like it too,' he said with a shrug.

'You never know,' added Ben. 'We might all get to use the honeymoon suite for the reason it was intended.'

'No chance of that with the kids around,' sighed Braindead.

'Perhaps we could babysit for each other a bit,' said Ben. 'Give us all a chance to have some couple time away from the kids.'

'I suppose,' said Braindead. 'Not that bothered, to be honest. I came here to have time with Logan and I'm sure if you asked Abby, she'd agree.'

Ben couldn't help thinking that by the look of Abby tonight, spending time with her son was the last thing she wanted to be doing on holiday.

Chapter Fourteen

'What are we going to do?' asked Katy, looking up at the podium where Abby was currently engaged in dancing around a pole.

'She's good,' said Daniel, 'really good. She should really think about doing that for a living.'

Katy turned to stare at him. 'Seriously!' she said. 'She is married, you know!'

'That's not looking like a woman with a husband up there at the moment,' he pointed out.

Katy looked back up and was horrified to see a man had joined her and was about to start writhing behind her.

'Oh God, Daniel, do something,' she said.

'Like what?'

'Go and stop him. He's such a letch and she's married. And she's so drunk, she doesn't know what she's doing.'

'Why have I got to step in?'

'Because, because you're a man. Can you imagine the fuss if I get up there? All the blokes will think it's lesbian hour or something, we could have a riot on our hands.'

Daniel looked at her disdainfully. 'You are *not* a convincing lesbian,' he said, looking at her sensible cotton dress. 'There is no-one here who would ever think that you were being brought on as entertainment in a lesbian show.'

'Thanks, Daniel. I shall consider later whether or not I should be offended by that statement but in the meantime will you get up there and help Abby?'

'She doesn't look like she needs help,' he said as Abby began to sway to the music with the topless man behind her.

'Well, if you won't do it for Abby, do it for Braindead,' she shouted in his ear.

'But he might hit me!' pleaded Daniel.

'So be subtle about it,' she said, giving him a push forward. He looked back at her pleadingly before stumbling towards the podium. She held her breath as he climbed up and then inched up behind the man. A massive cheer went up from the writhing crowd. Daniel looked around and a smile broke out on his face. He then caught sight of the pert buttocks of the man twisting and writhing behind Abby and so sidled up to him and mimicked his actions. Daniel looked like he was starting to enjoy his mission.

The crowd were now roaring their approval and Daniel was waving cheerily to his supporters whilst the man was still unaware that he was having the mickey taken out of him from behind.

Daniel carried on and the cheers grew and grew until the man looked up and noticed the entire throbbing dance floor was gazing up at him and laughing and cheering. He smiled for a moment and then became aware of something behind him. He looked over his shoulder to see a grinning Daniel pulling a face and aping his moves. The crowd's laughter increased and the man leapt off the stage and disappeared, a wave of back-patting following him.

Of course Daniel took the opportunity to take a bow to his appreciative audience. Then he tapped the oblivious Abby on the shoulder and indulged her in a brief dance before taking her hand and gently leading her off the stage back down to where Katy was standing.

My hero, Katy mouthed at her friend.

'For Braindead,' nodded Daniel.

'And for the adulation of about a thousand clubbers?' she asked.

He smiled. 'Not bad for an old-timer like me, hey. Now I think I've had way too much excitement for one evening,' he declared. 'Would it be acceptable to go home now? I've no idea where everyone else is so I reckon we could get away with a disappearing act right now, don't you think?'

'Absolutely,' agreed Katy. 'Come on, Abby,' she said. 'We're going home. Come on, let's go.'

'No!' said Abby. 'No way. It's early. I'll… I'll go and find Fi and Rachel. You go. I'll be back later.'

'But Abby, I really don't think it's a good idea to come back to the hotel on your own, do you? Why don't you come back with us now? We said we'd do the early shift with the kids in the morning as well, didn't we? Let the boys have a lie-in.'

Abby stared back at her blinking, processing her thoughts in a drunken stupor.

'No,' she said, shaking her head. 'I'm having fun. I won't go home yet.'

'Where have you been?' came a sudden screech from behind them as Fi and Rachel staggered up. 'We've been looking all over.'

'I had a dance on the podium,' said Abby proudly.

'Was that when everyone was cheering?' said Fi aghast. 'We couldn't see who it was.'

'Think so,' nodded Abby, grabbing hold of a stool to keep herself steady.

'So I think we're all going to go to the Calipo next,' announced Fi. 'They have a two-for-one from midnight.'

'Brilliant,' Abby said. 'I'll see you two later,' she added, turning to Katy and Daniel.

'You not coming?' asked Fi.

'They want to go home,' said Abby sulkily.

'Oh that's fine,' said Fi. 'We'll take care of Abby, won't we?'

'Will you?' said Katy, trying desperately hard not to sound like a disapproving mother.

'Of course,' said Fi.

'Will you bring her back to the hotel?' she asked. 'You won't let her walk back on her own, will you?' she urged, knowing any chance of trying to sound relaxed was gone.

'Yes, we'll bring her back,' nodded Fi, although Katy doubted whether she would remember anything about this conversation in five minutes' time.

'Or she can come back to ours and kip on our sofa if we can't find your hotel. No worries. It will be fine,' said Rachel. 'Now come on, we could miss the strippers if we're not careful. See you soon, guys,' she said, shouting over her shoulder and dragging Abby with her.

Katy was left open-mouthed, fighting the urge to go after her.

'Sometimes you've just got to let them go,' said Daniel. 'And just hope they come back.'

Katy stood shaking her head. 'What's Braindead going to say?' she said. 'What's he going to say if he wakes up tomorrow and she's not there? He's going to kill me.'

'It's not you he should be angry with,' said Daniel. 'It's Abby surely. She's a grown-up. What are you supposed to do? Demand she come home? You did what you could and now we can look forward to a day on the beach tomorrow with at least two people miserable and not talking to each other. Happy days, eh?'

'We should at least go and say goodbye to Cassie,' said Katy. 'Would be polite. And I want to see if she's okay.'

'Polite,' mused Daniel. 'An interesting word to use in association with a hen party.'

'Have I just shown my age?'

'Yet again,' sighed Daniel. 'Come on then, let's do the polite thing and then get out of here.'

'Can I just go to the loo first?' asked Katy.

'You've only just been!' he said, throwing his hands in the air.

'It's my age!' she said, smiling.

*

As nightclub toilets went, it wasn't too bad. Actually they were pretty impressive. The paint finish appeared to be a black matt emulsion embedded with glitter and giggling girls crowded round the enormous gilt-framed mirrors with backstage-dressing-room-level lighting.

Of course there was no lack of drama. A very blonde girl with the most impressive hair extensions stood at one end with mascara running rivers all down her face. She was surrounded by well-wishers saying things like, 'He always was a bastard,' and 'He'll do the same to her,' but nothing seemed to be abating the tear flow.

Katy slipped into a vacant toilet and was happy for a moment's peace. She took out her phone to see if there were any urgent messages coming through, which was of course extremely unlikely given the time of night, and then got distracted by the words #MassiveElephant trending on Twitter. On discovering it was not of that much interest at all, she realised she had been sitting there far too long and Daniel would be wondering where on earth she had got to.

She opened the door of the cubicle and nearly tripped over a pair of legs. Someone was sitting on the floor, leaning against the wall, staring at their phone.

'You might need to move before you trip someone up,' said Katy, looking down and realising it was Cassie. 'What are you doing down there, Cassie?' she asked.

Cassie looked up, startled.

'Are you FaceTiming your fiancé?' Katy asked her. 'You know Ruth will be very cross if she finds out you've been in touch. Isn't that one of the rules? You're not allowed to contact men at home in any shape or form. Especially not fiancés!'

Ruth had given the three of them a run-down of her hen party rules in the first bar. All of them seemed to be designed to make sure poor Cassie would have the worst time possible.

'I… I… I'm watching cat videos,' she said, turning the screen to show Katy.

Katy gasped. She didn't know what was more appalling. Cassie breaking Ruth's hen do rules by speaking to her fiancé or her sitting on the toilet floor on her hen do watching cat videos.

'Don't tell Ruth, will you?' she said looking desperate. 'She'll make me do some terrible forfeit or something. Please don't tell her.'

Katy shook her head. 'Of course I won't but I have to ask you, Cassie, why are you sat on the toilet floor in a nightclub watching cat videos?'

Cassie blinked back up at her and then to Katy's horror she watched as Cassie's eyes filled with tears.

What should she do now? Cassie showed no sign of getting up so she had no choice but to join her on the floor and put her arm around her.

'There's no need to cry,' said Katy. 'Really! The floor isn't even sticky.'

Cassie managed to raise a smile, then it disappeared and then she just looked really sad.

'So why are you here?' Katy asked again gently. 'Are you not enjoying your hen do?'

Cassie shook her head. 'Not really.'

'They're not everyone's cup of tea, are they?' continued Katy. 'Enforced drinking and dancing to Olivia Newton-John isn't for everyone.'

Cassie nodded.

Katy thought she sounded like a boring old woman. When had that happened? When had she stopped being the type of woman who enjoys a hen do? There was a time when she would have dropped everything for alcohol and dancing to Olivia Newton-John.

'I feel so bad,' said Cassie.

'It's not your fault,' said Katy. 'Do you know what? I reckon hen parties now are planned more for the guests than the bride-to-be. No-one really cares what she wants, they just want an excuse to go crazy.'

'But... but... I shouldn't even be on this hen night,' whimpered Cassie.

'What do you mean?'

Cassie looked up at her, stricken.

'Because,' she said, 'because I'm not sure...' She stopped and swallowed.

'Not sure about what?'

'Not sure if I want to get married.' Cassie looked up at her, searching Katy's face for reaction. Or perhaps she was searching for judgement.

Oh shit, thought Katy, trying very hard not to let her face react. Oh shit, what should she say now? Why was Cassie telling her this?

She hardly knew the poor girl. But then she thought about how Ruth or someone like Fi would react and it made perfect sense that Cassie was telling her.

'It's perfectly normal to have doubts,' said Katy, trying desperately to string some sensible words together. 'Especially now when it's all about to happen. It's just cold feet,' she said. 'That's all.'

Cassie nodded as if Katy was getting it right. As if somehow she had managed to say the right thing.

'I wake up in the middle of the night in cold sweats,' said Cassie. 'I keep having this reoccurring nightmare that I hate being married to Jules so much that I strangle him with my bare hands.'

'You dream of strangling him?' said Katy, trying to keep the astonishment out of her voice.

'Yes,' she nodded. 'Apart from the time I drowned him. In the bath in our flat.'

Katy nodded as she gave careful consideration to these violent manifestations of Cassie's wedding cold feet.

'Did you ever have doubts?' asked Cassie.

'Yes,' said Katy. 'It's such a huge decision that it's hard not to.'

'Did you ever dream of killing your future husband and burying him in the back garden?'

'You also buried him?' said Katy, unable this time to cover her shock.

'Yes,' said Cassie. 'In my dad's garden using his spade. My dad's not very keen on Jules so I wondered if that was why I chose his spade to dig the hole.'

'Mmmm,' said Katy nodding her head. 'Makes sense.'

Cassie sighed and fiddled with the trim on her top.

'Have you told Jules you dream about killing him?' asked Katy.

Cassie shook her head. 'He'd be devastated,' she said.

Katy found herself longing for that boring family holiday she had been half dreading. God, she was tired. She needed to go to bed.

'Do you love him?' she said, turning to look at Cassie.

'What?' asked Cassie, looking startled.

'Do you love him? Simple question.'

Cassie didn't answer straight away. She looked away first and didn't even make eye contact when she gave her reply.

'I think so,' she mumbled.

Shit! thought Katy. This marriage is doomed.

'Not a great answer,' she ventured.

'I'm not even sure I know what love is,' said Cassie, looking up at her this time.

Katy took a deep breath.

'May I suggest,' said Katy softly. 'That if you are not sure what love is then you are probably not in love with Jules and actually that might indicate that you should perhaps take these nightmares seriously.'

Katy's heartbeat was going very fast now. She was on such dangerous territory. She was suggesting that someone call off their wedding. Someone she barely knew.

'What are you saying?' asked Cassie.

Oh no, thought Katy. Cassie wanted her to spell it out. How was this happening? She should be tucked up in bed now next to two snoring kids, not sitting on the floor of a nightclub trying to prevent someone from possibly ruining their own life, and definitely ruining someone else's.

Katy opened her mouth to speak but shut it at the last minute. She didn't know Cassie well enough to be blunt. What if this was just drunken ramblings that she was in danger of taking too seriously?

'What are you afraid of?' she eventually asked. Answer a hard question with another question, she thought. She'd watched Daniel squirm out of many an awkward patch using that strategy.

Cassie stared back at her.

'Letting everyone down,' she replied. 'There's a non-refundable deposit on the venue and the wedding car.'

'It's just money,' said Katy.

'It will destroy Jules,' she added.

'Will it?' asked Katy.

Cassie nodded.

'Would it destroy him more to have you marry him and then divorce him in a few years' time because you are unhappy? Oh, I forgot you're going to drown him first, aren't you?'

Cassie managed to raise a small smile.

'Thank you,' she said.

'What for?' asked Katy.

'For listening and not shouting at me.'

'Look,' said Katy. 'Daniel and I are going to head back. We're old, you know. Why don't we walk you back to your hotel? I think you've got some thinking to do.'

'Would you?' said Cassie, looking hopeful for the first time. 'I'm really not enjoying myself.'

'Sure,' said Katy. 'Let's go and tell the rest we are going so they don't send out a search party and then I think we all need to sleep on it.'

*

'We're going to go, Ruth,' said Katy as they approached her at the bar. Katy had told Daniel that she'd found Cassie in the toilets and they'd lost track of time talking. Cassie had made her swear not to tell anyone about her doubts. 'Too old for all this,' Katy said to Ruth, casting her hand around the mayhem. 'Thanks so much for inviting us though. Really, it's been a blast.'

'Right, let's go,' said Cassie, pulling on her hand behind her. 'Let's go *now.*'

But it was not to be. She got her timing completely wrong as just at that moment Ruth got her trusty whistle out and the dulcet tones of Olivia Newton-John could be heard over Ariana Grande as the remaining members of the hen party quickly gathered.

'You go,' urged Cassie, catching sight of the looks of horror on Katy and Daniel's faces. 'Honestly. I know you don't want to do this again. Thanks for everything.' She smiled weakly and turned to join the rest of the party before Ruth blew her whistle again.

'Come on,' said Daniel, pulling on Katy's sleeve. 'Quick or else Ruth will drag us into it again. Come on, quick, run!'

He grabbed her hand and they made a dash for it, pushing past the lager drinkers and the cocktail guzzlers, ducking and diving, gathering speed until they made their way out into the open air outside the club. Katy could feel her heart going like the clappers as she looked nervously over her shoulder in case Ruth had followed them out, still worried about Cassie.

They stood clutching each other, trying to grab a breath.

'Well, that was weird,' said Daniel eventually. 'How on earth did we get involved in that? Bloody budget airlines and having to sit next to strangers on the plane. I'm never flying like that again.'

'You were the one who got chatting. You were the one buying them drinks. You can't blame the airline. You got involved of your own free will. We're just past all this stuff.'

'Thank goodness,' he nodded. 'I never ever ever ever want to perform a dance on demand of a whistle ever again. Right now I just want to climb in bed with my husband and… and… well, I guess we will have to sleep. Bloody hell, what kind of holiday is this?'

Chapter Fifteen

Daniel had made every effort not to wake Gabriel or Silvie when he got in. He took his shoes off then opened the door inch by inch, trying not to make a sound. He shed his clothes in the tight hallway without even turning on the lights, knowing that the slightest sound could wake their daughter and that was the last thing they both needed at this time of night.

He tiptoed across the room and jumped straight into his single bed, chuntering under his breath at the unfairness of their sleeping arrangements. He could just about make out Gabriel's body in the next bed, rising and falling, before he closed his eyes and prayed he didn't have room-spin. Sleep came quickly.

*

'Fuck… fuck… fuck, what the hell, what are you doing here?' cried Daniel as he came out of the bathroom the next morning, having marvelled at the fact they had all had a lie-in and no-one had stirred before seven thirty. He'd walked out of the bathroom to be faced with Ollie sitting up in Gabriel's bed, rubbing his eyes, as he stood there naked.

*

'I'm not speaking to anyone,' announced Daniel when he later made it down to the beach. He was clutching a miserable-looking Silvie in a baby sling on his chest, having eventually tracked down Gabriel and his daughter in the honeymoon suite. He was wearing dark shades and his linen shirt was starting to look crumpled as well as his hair being all askew.

'You got a hangover too?' asked Ben, who was digging a hole in the sand with Millie.

'I have not got a hangover,' protested Katy, bouncing Jack up and down on her knee. 'I'm just tired, really very tired. And this one woke up screaming at six thirty so is it any wonder I feel like death?'

'Mummy,' said Jack, giving her a winning smile and banging his hand into her mouth.

'It's okay to be all smiles now,' she said to him. 'Why couldn't you have been like this at the crack of dawn?'

'Well, at least you didn't have the shock of your life this morning when you came out of the bathroom only to find a strange man in your bedroom,' announced Daniel.

'What!' said Ben and Katy.

'A man!' exclaimed Daniel. 'Sitting on the bed.'

'Oh my God, who?' asked Katy. 'How did they get in, have you contacted security? Was Silvie with you?'

'Well,' said Daniel, laying Silvie carefully on a lounger and plonking the nappy rucksack on the sand. 'No need as I knew him.'

'Knew him!' exclaimed Katy. 'But I only left you on the second floor, did you manage to pull on the way to the bedroom? Oh Daniel, tell me that you didn't.'

'Of course I bloody didn't. Apparently Gabriel won the honeymoon suite from Ollie in a game of table football last night and so they swapped rooms before we got back but failed to tell me and so I crept into the room oblivious. I not only had the shock of my life this morning but also missed a night's sleep in a kingsize bed *with my husband*. Unbelievable.'

'They said they were going to leave you a big note on the door,' said Ben.

'Well, I can't say I was up to reading any notes at that time of night. I didn't see a thing. But to be honest, I think Ollie is more traumatised than I am. He thought it would do him good to get out of the bridal suite but he didn't bank on his new bedroom coming with a flash of my naked body.'

'Holy Moly,' said Ben laughing. 'As if this holiday could get any worse for the poor lad.'

'Hey,' said Daniel. 'I'm in good nick, I'll have you know. Just not what he would be expecting to write on his postcards home.'

'So have you deposited yourself in the honeymoon suite now?' asked Ben.

'Oh yes,' said Daniel. 'I've left Gabriel there for a lie-in. Nearly broke my heart.'

'Where is she?' they suddenly heard being shouted behind them.

They all turned to see Braindead dashing down the sand towards them, Logan clasped to his chest.

'Did she sleep in one of your rooms?' he demanded. 'Did she?'

Daniel glanced over at Katy and then pretended to study the sand.

'We left her at the club,' started Katy, realising immediately how terrible that sounded.

'You did what?' said Braindead.

'She wanted to stay out and we'd had enough and two of the girls in the group said they would look after her. Said they'd bring her home. Promised they wouldn't leave her on her own.'

'You left her?' he said in astonishment. 'How could you do that?'

'She wanted to stay,' said Katy. 'I couldn't tell her to come back. I'm not her mother.'

'Look, Braindead,' said Daniel. 'She was having a great time, there was no way we could have persuaded her to come home. We did try.'

To Katy's horror she watched as Braindead's eyes flooded with tears.

'But she didn't come back, did she?' he spluttered. 'I woke up with Logan at two a.m. and just thought she'd gone for a late one, but she still hadn't come back this morning. And Logan's not even had his breakfast yet. What do I do, look for my wife or feed my son?'

'Have you tried phoning her?' asked Ben.

'Of course. I had a message from her just before midnight. But I think she butt-called me. It was just loud music, no talking. I tried calling her as soon as I woke up but there was no answer. I don't know if her phone is dead or something.'

'Give Logan to me,' said Ben, standing up and taking Logan from him. 'I'll take this one for breakfast and you and Katy and Daniel track Abby down. Can you keep digging next to Mummy, Millie?' he asked his daughter. 'I'll come back soon to help you build the wall.'

Millie didn't answer, just kept digging.

'You can call someone from the hen party, can't you?' Ben said, turning to Katy.

'Yes, of course,' she replied. This was her worst nightmare. Well, second worst. Mislaying one of the children of course was her worst nightmare but her husband's best mate's wife was not far behind.

'Good,' said Ben, in a pull-yourself-together type of tone. 'So you fancy some pancakes, buddy?' he said to Logan.

'Yes,' Logan cried in delight as they disappeared off back to the hotel.

'I'm ringing Ruth now,' said Daniel. Katy looked over to see his phone pressed to his ear.

'You have Ruth's number?' Katy asked in surprise.

'She insisted,' he replied. 'She programmed it in herself on the plane.'

'Is she picking up?' asked Braindead urgently, almost grabbing the phone off him.

'It's just rang out,' replied Daniel.

'Try again,' urged Katy. 'She might just be ignoring you.'

He tapped the relevant buttons again.

They all waited with bated breath.

'She's not answering,' he said. 'And I need to change Silvie's nappy.'

'Can we go in the sea?' said Millie. 'I need to get some more shells.'

'No hitting, Millie,' whinged Jack. 'Stop, Millie.'

'Call her again,' demanded Braindead, putting his hands on his hips.

'Will you change Silvie's nappy then?' Daniel asked Braindead.

'Can we see if my wife is still alive before wiping poo off your daughter's arse?' said Braindead, clearly beginning to get angry.

'Don't use that expression in relation to my daughter,' said Daniel.

'What, poo?' said Braindead.

'No, arse,' said Daniel.

'What's wrong with arse?' demanded Braindead.

'She's a baby,' said Daniel. 'She's Silvie. She does not have, and will never have, an arse.'

'Boys!' said Katy. 'This isn't getting us anywhere.'

'Can we go in the sea, Mummy?' asked Millie again. 'And I didn't hit Jack again before he says. I just held his arm. He doesn't know the difference yet because he's only a toddler.'

'Just ring the number again,' demanded Braindead.

'Millie!' said Katy, shouting at her daughter. 'Do not hit Jack. Why are you hitting Jack?'

'Millie stop,' said Jack. 'Stop.'

'Owww!' shouted Millie.

'Do not hit her back,' said Katy to Jack.

'She hit me,' squealed Jack.

Millie started crying real tears. Drops flooding down her cheeks. 'He hit me,' she sobbed. 'Really hard. You saw him, didn't you, Mummy? You saw him hit me.'

'Is she picking up?' Braindead asked Daniel, the phone now pressed back against his ear.

'If she had picked up, do you not think I would have told you?' grimaced Daniel. 'Do you think I would be just ignoring her as she's gabbing away to me on the phone whilst I pretend she hasn't answered? Is that what you think?' He pulled the phone away from his ear again and shrugged. 'She's not picking up,' he announced.

'Then do something!' declared Braindead, running his hands through his hair.

'What exactly do you want us to do?' asked Daniel.

'Find her,' he demanded. 'You lost her,' he added accusingly. 'You need to find her.'

'We didn't lose her, Braindead,' said Daniel. 'She just didn't want to come home with us. We couldn't make her. We're *not* her parents.'

'But you promised you'd look after her,' protested Braindead.

'But what were we supposed to do?' asked Katy. 'We made sure she wasn't going to come back alone. Rachel and Fi promised they would stay with her. She must have gone back to their hotel with them. She must have, mustn't she?' she said to Daniel.

'Of course she has,' said Daniel, picking up Silvie. He slung the nappy bag over his shoulder. 'Now, if you'll excuse me, I have some real shit to deal with…'

'I'm sorry, Braindead,' said Katy as Daniel walked off. 'We really did try to get her to come back with us.'

'I know,' said Braindead, sitting down on Daniel's lounger with a thump. 'I... I... just... just don't know what to do, Katy.'

Katy wanted to get up and throw her arms around Braindead and would have done if not for the fact that Jack was currently bashing her with a spade and Millie had scrambled onto her lap and was about to hit Jack over the head with a bucket.

'Stop that, Jack,' she said, pushing him away. 'And don't you dare put that bucket over your brother's head,' she said to her daughter. 'Do you have any idea how dangerous that is?'

'Abby!' she suddenly heard Braindead shout.

Katy looked up to see a dishevelled-looking Abby stumbling down the beach towards them. She had on the same dress as she was wearing when she went out the night before, her shoes were dangling from one hand and her phone was clasped in the other. Her face was slightly red raw as though she had washed it with soap and water, and tinges of mascara clung desperately around her eyes. Her expression was blank. Katy searched Abby's face for signs of contrition but there was nothing. Absolutely nothing.

'Thank goodness you're back. I was worried,' said Braindead. 'Why didn't you answer your phone?'

'Ran out of battery,' she stated, falling down onto a lounger. 'Sometime last night. Probably about three o'clock. Fi didn't have a charger.' She leaned back on the lounger and closed her eyes, as though explanations were done with. That was all she had to say.

'But what about Logan?' Braindead blurted out.

Katy wanted to get up and leave. This was a private conversation but the chances of her getting away discreetly were zero with two children in tow.

'What about Logan?' asked Abby. 'He's fine, isn't he?'

'Yes, but…' said Braindead. 'I was worried.'

Abby didn't reply, just turned onto her side and tucked her hands under her cheek as though settling down to sleep.

Braindead glanced over to Katy, who looked away quickly. She didn't need to be involved in this.

There was a long silence.

'Thought we might hire one of those paddle boats later,' he said eventually. 'Take this little chappie out on one. What about it? You, me and Logan out on the open seas together.'

Abby opened one eye to look at Braindead, considered him for a moment and then sat up.

'I need sleep,' she said, going pale as she said it. 'I'm going back to the room.' She got up and grabbed her shoes.

'Okay, but what about ice cream later then?' said Braindead, as she turned to go. 'I think Logan's got his eye on trying a Magnum.'

'Sure,' Abby nodded. She looked sad and opened her mouth to say something but changed her mind. She turned to walk away.

*

It was three o'clock by the time Abby reappeared. All the make-up was gone and she was dressed down in cotton shorts and a T-shirt. She looked drained; she looked worn down, in fact. She gave Braindead a weak smile as she approached him on the beach.

'You ready for an ice cream then?' she said.

'Yeah, course, cool. We've held off having one, haven't we, Logan, so we could wait for Mummy. Do you want to hang out here with Logan whilst I go and fetch them? What do you fancy?'

'Er, you choose,' she said.

'Great,' said Braindead. 'I'll get you a surprise then. Back in a tick.'

Braindead bounded off in the direction of the hut located towards the back of the beach, relieved that they were finally managing to do something together as a family. He had vivid memories of his childhood holidays with his mum and dad where his dad would make him wait all day until they were allowed an ice cream on Cleethorpes Beach. He and his sister would beg to be allowed one earlier but his parents never gave in. He wasn't going to be like that with Logan – if he wanted an ice cream, he could have an ice cream.

The queue was quite long and Braindead kept looking back nervously. Abby was now digging in the sand with Logan. For some reason it made him feel quite emotional. Tears sprang to his eyes as he watched his wife playing with his son on the sand. His wife and his son. He could barely believe it. It also made him think of his mother who had died when he was fifteen. He tried to bring back memories of playing in the sand but he couldn't. Maybe they never did. He wished they had so he could remember it now.

'Here you go,' he said, handing a Solero over to Abby and sitting down on the floor so he could unwrap Logan's Magnum for him. 'Now are you ready for this, young man?' he said to his son. 'This is a big moment for me and your mum. See you have your first Magnum. Isn't that right, Abby?'

Abby merely raised her eyebrows and sank her teeth into her ice cream.

'So I'm going to hand it over and then you need to wait just a moment whilst I get my phone out so I can take a picture, you got that?'

Logan nodded solemnly as Braindead handed the ice cream over to him.

Braindead looked away to rummage in his bag and dig out his phone, turning back when he had found it and clicking on the camera app.

'What did you let him do that for!' he gasped when he saw that Logan had already dropped his ice cream. It was already covered in sand and looked like a sinking ship.

'What?' said Abby, who had been busy gazing out to sea.

'He dropped it,' he said, grasping for it and attempting to brush the sand off.

'I'm sorry, I… I… wasn't watching,' said Abby.

'I'll have to go and buy him another one now,' said Braindead.

'He can have mine,' said Abby. 'No big deal.'

'But it's not a Magnum!'

'So?'

'I wanted a picture of him trying his first Magnum.'

'Well, it looks like he's quite happy with my Solero.'

'But it's not a Magnum, is it?'

'Does it matter?'

'Yes, it does.'

'Fine, go and buy him another Magnum then,' huffed Abby.

'Why are you so mad at me?' exclaimed Braindead.

'Because it's ridiculous. He's got no idea what a Magnum is so it really doesn't matter.'

'All I'm doing is trying to create some happy holiday memories,' declared Braindead. 'You know, stuff he might remember. Stuff I remember, like eating ice cream with my mum and dad on the pier at three o'clock on the dot every day and my dad saying, "Well, that was worth waiting for, wasn't it?"'

Abby stared back at him.

'All I remember about our family holidays,' she said, 'is being left in a crappy hotel bedroom every night to babysit my brother whilst Mum and Dad went out.'

'Oh,' said Braindead.

'I hated family holidays,' she continued. 'Couldn't wait until I could go away with my mates.'

'Right,' said Braindead. He gazed out to sea wondering how on earth he was going to retrieve the situation.

'I, er, booked us all on a day trip tomorrow, by the way,' he added after the awkward pause. 'Exclusive private beach and barbeque just up the coast. Oh, and they said they also provide some amazing local entertainment. Should be great. Logan's going to love it.'

Abby nodded. 'If you think he should have another Magnum then go and get him one,' she said eventually.

'I think I will,' said Braindead, getting up. 'You all right here whilst I have another go?'

'Yeah,' she said, picking up Logan's spade with a long sigh.

Chapter Sixteen

Ben wasn't really looking forward to his night of freedom any more, especially when he arrived down at the bar to meet Braindead and Ollie and saw the really miserable looks on both of their faces. Katy had told him to let his hair down. Have a good time. He deserved it. But the truth was that he was knackered. Right at this moment he would have swapped a night out on the beers for a full night's sleep any day of the week.

Gabriel had shown them all up by persuading Katy to babysit Silvie so that he and Daniel could enjoy a night alone together. They had virtually skipped out of the hotel on their way to a restaurant for a meal with just the two of them. 'Without a high chair or pelican bib in sight,' Daniel had declared joyfully as he kissed Silvie on the head before they left her in Katy's arms as Abby tried to organise something on the iPad to keep Millie, Jack and Logan amused.

So the boys' night out was all down to Ben. He had to be the key motivator this evening. The one to get everyone's spirits up. The one to help find Ollie a holiday romance somewhere in the midst of this sea of 'young people' that were out there frequenting the bars and clubs outside of the family resort they were hiding in. The one to stop Braindead pining for his son and the family holiday ideal that was not happening due to his wife's defection to a hen party. He took a deep breath and stifled a yawn.

'So, comrades,' he said, slapping them both on the back. 'Are we ready to take this town by storm?' he asked.

They both groaned.

'Down those drinks and let's head out.'

*

Twenty minutes later they were sitting in the Irish bar surrounded by men watching golf on huge screens. They barely spoke to each other for at least an hour apart from to say, 'Pint?' There was a play-off, for which all three of them were grateful. Another three holes during which they didn't have to talk to each other, didn't have to make conversation. Just watch a screen and drink pints.

But inevitably someone did win and lifted a trophy, leaving them staring at each other, knowing that the night's main event could be put off no longer. Ben felt the weight of the responsibility heavy on his shoulders. He would do anything for one of them to say, 'Shall we just head home and have an early night?'

'Shall we just head home and have an early night?' suggested Ollie.

Thank the lord, thought Ben, he'd be in bed within the half hour with a bit of luck.

'What do you mean, have an early night?' said Braindead, as though someone had just shot him through with adrenaline. His eyes were wide and staring, a look of incredulity on his face. 'We're out, out,' he continued. 'Boys out together on the lash. We have a free pass.' He looked around him as though he had noticed his surroundings for the first time. 'And what are we doing still in here? It's full of blokes. We're not going to find a nice young lady for Ollie in the Irish bar, are we? Look at these losers. They're only in here because they know they haven't got a cat in hell's chance of pulling. Ugly twats.'

'Bloody hell, Braindead,' said Ben, hustling him out. 'Talk about taking your life into your own hands.'

Ollie stumbled after them. 'You don't have to take me out, you know,' he said.

'Yes, we do,' declared Braindead grimly. 'Yes, we do.'

*

'What about her?' said Braindead fifteen minutes later when they found themselves in a packed bar with a jumping dance floor. Ben had spent ten minutes trying to get a drink whilst Braindead and Ollie cased the joint. Ben arrived back with three bottles of Bud.

'What's this crap?' asked Braindead, looking incredulously at the bottles of lager.

'No beer, mate, and I didn't fancy my chances walking through this lot with three plastic pints in my hands. So sup this and shut up.'

'Thanks, Ben,' said Ollie, taking a swig and then looking around nervously.

'So?' asked Ben. 'Any useful sightings?'

'It's a horror show,' said Braindead. 'I can't look,' he added, shielding his eyes. 'They're all semi-naked and… and… young… and I feel like a complete letch. I want to keep pointing at Ollie and saying, "I'm with him, I'm married with a baby. Please ignore me."'

'What about you?' Ben asked Ollie.

He shrugged. 'I just don't know where to start. I'm really not sure if this is a good idea.'

'No,' said Braindead. 'Come on. We need to get you back in the game. Her over there, look. She's on her own. She looks a bit lost. She looks achievable.'

'Achievable?' questioned Ollie.

'You know, not so pretty that she's just going to laugh in your face,' said Braindead, taking another swig of his bottle. 'I'd say she was on your level.'

Ollie looked over and studied her.

'I'm sure she's lovely but she's kind of short,' he said.

Braindead stared back at him. 'You're not exactly Big Ben,' he commented.

'Are you calling me short?' asked Ollie.

'Well, yes,' said Braindead. 'You're never going to pull an Elle Macpherson, are you?'

'I've never considered my height to be an issue,' said Ollie. 'Is it an issue? I've never even thought about it. Ellie was shorter than me. Shit, I'm doomed, aren't I?'

'No!' said Ben, blowing his cheeks out. 'Forget about it. Just be you. Why don't you just go over and ask her if you can buy her a drink?'

'What, just like that?' said Ollie.

'Yes,' he nodded.

'But what if she doesn't want a drink? What if she's waiting for a friend to bring her a drink? What if she wants one of those really expensive cocktails and she asks me to get her one and then walks off?'

Braindead gave Ollie a hard shove in the direction of the girl. 'Go and ask her if she wants a drink!' he urged.

Ollie stumbled towards the girl, looking back at them with a vicious stare as though they were the school bullies and they'd asked him to go and shoplift in the newsagents.

They watched as he turned a smile on the girl and began talking to her.

'Do you think we'll be doing this with Jack and Logan one day?' Ben said to Braindead.

'What? Out on the piss encouraging them to try and have sex with girls?' asked Braindead.

'I wouldn't have put it like that,' replied Ben. 'I meant out on a night out, having a beer with them.'

'How old will we be by the time they are eighteen?' asked Braindead.

'I guess early fifties,' replied Ben.

'What!' exclaimed Braindead, turning to look at him. 'You have to be kidding me. We can't be?'

'We can,' said Ben.

'I can't be in my fifties that soon?'

'It's coming, mate, believe me.'

'Guys?' said Ollie, suddenly appearing at their side with the girl in tow. She looked somewhat reluctant. 'She couldn't hear a word I said because we were right next to a speaker,' he shouted at them.

'Okay,' nodded Ben encouragingly.

No-one said anything.

'So are you going to ask her then?' said Ben.

Ollie had gone a puce colour and the girl was looking round desperately.

'Ask her what?' said Ollie.

Jesus, thought Ben. 'You know, that question we said you should ask her?'

Ollie stared back at him and then appeared to wake up. 'Oh yeah,' he said, turning to look at her. 'Do you think I'm short?'

The girl screwed her eyes up, shook her head and walked off.

'What the hell was that?' asked Braindead.

'What?' said Ollie, looking as though he was about to burst into tears. 'Isn't that what I should have said?'

'You were meant to ask her if you could buy her a drink!' said Ben.

'Oh yeah,' said Ollie, putting his head in his hands. 'I... I... I just panicked. I told you I was rubbish. I've never had to do it, you see. I told you I've only been out with Ellie and she asked me out. I just don't know what to do.'

Ben and Braindead looked at each other over Ollie's head. 'Dance floor,' declared Braindead. 'No need to talk. Just dance and look into their eyes.'

'I can't dance,' said Ollie. 'I don't dance. Ellie said I danced like a giraffe.'

'Did she mean a giraffe?' asked Braindead. 'I mean, they are tall, you know.'

'Enough of this short thing,' said Ollie. 'You're going to give me a complex. Anyway I don't dance, seriously.'

'Rubbish,' said Ben. 'Come on, we'll come with you. We must be at least ten years older than everyone else on the dance floor so we'll be the ones looking like idiots, not you, so come on. Get your wiggle on.'

*

Ben and Braindead stared in awe at Ollie. Never had they seen a more uncoordinated, unrhythmic set of body movements in their life. It was David Brent... no, it was far worse than David Brent. Far, far worse. They'd ignored him for a while until they became aware of a space opening up behind them and looked back to see the impressively bad dancer that was Ollie. He had his eyes closed in concentration fortunately, so he couldn't see the stares and the pointing and the giggling that was coming from around him.

'We need to get him out of here,' said Ben, shaking his head.

'How is he actually doing that?' asked Braindead, cocking his head to one side in awe.

'I have no idea but we really need to get out of here now before we are banished from this town!'

They descended on Ollie, grabbing an arm each, and led him off the dance floor as he looked around, bewildered. Moments later, they were out on the pavement outside the bar.

'It was bad, wasn't it?' said Ollie.

Ben and Braindead looked away.

'You don't have to say anything,' said Ollie, shaking his head. 'Do you want to know something? I'm that bad at dancing that Ellie made me promise that we wouldn't do a first dance at our wedding. She said it wasn't worth the humiliation and she wanted to be able to still walk by the end of the night.'

'Are you serious?' asked Braindead. 'She was too embarrassed to do a first dance with you on your wedding day?'

'You've seen me,' said Ollie. 'Wouldn't you be?'

Braindead looked at him.

'I wouldn't care,' he said. 'On my wedding day I would have my first dance whatever. No-one can laugh at your dancing on your wedding day. You can do what you like then.'

Ollie said nothing.

'Sorry, mate,' said Braindead, touching his arm. 'Look, maybe if she was too embarrassed to dance with you on your wedding day then it wasn't meant to be. She clearly didn't love you enough if she wouldn't dance with you.'

'Braindead!' exclaimed Ben. 'Ignore him, Ollie. He hasn't a clue what he's saying.'

'I know exactly what I am saying,' said Braindead.

'He's right,' said Ollie, looking away.

'No, he's not,' said Ben. 'He talks utter bullshit half the time. Believe me, I've known him practically all my life.'

'But he's right though, isn't he?' said Ollie. 'She didn't love me enough. It's as simple as that. She didn't love me enough to marry me, never mind dance with me.'

They stood looking at each other as the tourist crowd seethed around them.

'Her loss, mate,' said Ben eventually.

'Yeah,' agreed Braindead. 'Her loss.'

'I always knew she didn't,' said Ollie, shaking his head. 'Deep down. I knew we were kind of together because it was easy rather than because of any great passion. She wanted a boyfriend at fourteen and I was there. I was just *there*. Then somehow we never found enough of a reason to end it. I was good to her. Treated her really well. You know. Really well.'

'I bet you remembered her birthday and everything, didn't you?' nodded Braindead.

'Of course and all the anniversaries.'

'Anniversaries?'

'Yeah, you know, like, first kiss, first time we had sex...'

'You celebrated the anniversary of the first time you had sex?' said Ben incredulously.

'Yeah, of course.'

'How?' asked Braindead.

'By having sex of course,' shrugged Ollie.

'Ah,' nodded Braindead. 'A cunning plan. At least once a year then. A good anniversary to uphold.'

'Well, it did happen to happen on her sixteenth birthday so, you know, it wasn't hard to remember.'

'So you celebrated her birthday and your sexiversary on the same day?' asked Ben.

'Yeah,' he nodded.

'Did that mean you had to buy two cards?' asked Braindead.

'No!' said Ollie. 'I didn't send her a sexiversary card. We just used to have sex. To begin with in the woods behind her house because that was where we first did it, but by our third sexiversary she requested we book a hotel.'

'Sensible,' nodded Ben.

'Good job I'd never heard of these sexiversaries when I lost my virginity or else I'd be having sex once a year in the bus shelter on the Hanley Road,' announced Braindead.

'I'd be in my old single bed at my mum and dad's house,' said Ben. 'They've still got that bed. Can you imagine making an excuse every year to go stay over at your mum and dad's so you could celebrate your sexiversary?'

'Embarrassing,' muttered Braindead.

'You'll find someone who loves you enough,' said Ben after a few moments of contemplation.

'That's easy for you to say,' said Ollie, giving a huge sigh. 'You've found yours. You've found the women who will love you whatever your faults are even if you are a shit dancer. You got your women down the aisle. That's it now, you are done with all this bollocks,' he added, casting his arm round at the cattle market that swelled around them. 'You don't have to be out there any more. You're secure and can be just who you please. Now I have to go out there and be somebody. Somebody who somebody might take a shine to. Not just myself.'

'You can be yourself,' protested Braindead.

'But myself wasn't enough, was it?' said Ollie.

'It wasn't enough for her,' said Ben. 'Doesn't mean it won't be enough for someone else.'

'If you say so,' shrugged Ollie.

*

By ten forty-five they were back in the hotel bar virtually sitting in the same seats that they had vacated only a few hours ago. Except by now the bar was buzzing from the karaoke machine that had been set up in the corner. Overtired kids were screeching into the microphone, followed by granddads who clearly had been told in their youth that they had a talent and still believed they had it as they elbowed small children out of the way in order to have their moment of glory.

'Can you sing?' said Ben, nudging Ollie.

'A bit. Why?'

'You should try it. Can work wonders with the ladies.'

'Yeah,' said Braindead. 'That's right. I mean, look at Ed Sheeran. He's got nothing going for him, has he really? But he can sing.'

Ollie cast his eye around the room. 'Not sure there's anyone in this hotel that would be interested,' he muttered. 'It's all couples and families. Have you noticed? I bet there's not one single person in here apart from me. Clearly it's bad policy to mix the single people with the couples – maybe we singles are not to be trusted. Like I'm a danger to anyone's happiness!'

'He'll have a go,' said Braindead, shouting a rep over. 'He's a regular George Ezra, I'm telling you. Go on, Ollie. Let's see you redeem yourself from that terrible dancing earlier.'

'Seriously?' said Ollie.

'Please,' said the rep, walking up to Ollie. 'Or else we'll have to have Harry on again and he's already been on four times tonight. He says he was once a backing singer for Ken Dodd. He reckons he's got a pair of Ken's underpants at home. Stole them when they were on a cruise ship together apparently. He's been on *Antiques Roadshow* with them twice.'

'Go on,' said Braindead to Ollie. 'You don't know anybody. What have you got to lose?'

Ollie gave a big sigh and slid off his stool onto the floor, stumbling his way to the karaoke machine, where he chatted with the man behind the machine before approaching the microphone.

'He's quite pissed, you know,' said Ben. 'Hope he's all right.'

'He'll be fine. Good sing-song always cheers me up.'

They heard a tapping and turned to see Ollie bashing the top of the microphone.

'Hello, hello,' he said, tapping away. 'Hello.'

'This might be a mistake,' said Ben.

'This is for all you lovers out there,' said Ollie, pointing around the room. 'If you are next to your loved one, reach out and take their hand and hold it tight because… because you don't know how lucky you are. That's it. Hold their hands really tight for me now because, you see, I lost my lover. I lost her.'

A collective 'Aaah' emerged from the crowd as they all paused to hear Ollie's tale of woe.

'Do you think they all think he means his lover died?' hissed Braindead.

'God, I hope not. We don't need everyone going up to him afterwards and commiserating with him for his loss.'

'I guess it's the same thing though, isn't it?' said Braindead. 'I mean, when you split up with someone. It's a bit like grief. They may as well have died.'

'Not sure that's helpful to think of it like that though, is it?' said Ben. 'Especially for Ollie. Jesus, is he crying?'

Ollie had his head in his hands as the opening bars of his chosen song started to strike up.

'He hasn't, has he?' said Ben, recognising the opening bars.

'Hasn't what?'

'Chosen what I think he's chosen. Yes, he has. Oh no, I can't bear to look.'

Ollie took his hands away from his face and began the mournful telling of Celine Dion's classic hit for the sad and lonely, 'All By Myself'.

'Do we let him do it?' said Braindead. 'No, we can't let him do it, can we?' he added, jumping off his stool. 'Come on, we don't have any choice.'

'Where are we going?'

'Come on,' he urged.

Ben gulped a mouthful of beer and followed Braindead down towards Ollie. We can't just drag him off the stage, he thought, but then something even worse occurred to him. Was Braindead serious? Yes, he was. He watched in horror as he picked up two spare microphones and handed one to Ben. He turned to face the audience, slinging one arm over Ollie's shoulders to join in with him just as he reached the chorus. Of course Ben had no option but to join them, the three of them linking arms as they faced their fellow holidaymakers, tears streaming down Ollie's cheeks. This wasn't how Ben had expected his holiday to pan out.

*

'You all right, mate?' Ben asked Braindead later after they had put Ollie to bed fully clothed and comatose.

'Yeah, why shouldn't I be?' he said.

'Well, it's not the holiday you were expecting, is it? Putting drunken men to bed at night and your wife having more fun on a stranger's hen party than building sandcastles.'

Braindead said nothing for a moment.

'I just don't get it,' he said eventually. 'Why does she need to go out with that lot when she's got me and Logan? Why wouldn't you want to spend every single moment with that boy? I mean, he's the business. I just don't understand what she's doing. I know where I'd rather be.'

Ben slung his arm around his shoulder.

'Perhaps this day trip you've organised for us all tomorrow will give you some family time together,' he said.

'Hope so,' said Braindead, shrugging. 'A secluded private beach and our own barbeque. What's not to love? I'm hoping it will make Abby realise that family holidays can be just as much fun as hen parties.'

'Of course it will,' said Ben. 'It's going to be great. It's exactly what everyone needs on this holiday. A great day out together.'

Chapter Seventeen

'I can't believe I'm going on a *day trip*,' said Daniel, approaching the rest of the gang gathered on the pavement outside the hotel the next day.

'What's wrong with a day trip?' asked Katy.

'It's the words, it's the sound of it, it's everything,' said Daniel. 'I can't go back to Leeds and tell them I went on a *day trip*. Old people go on day trips. Old people who have no imagination so rely on other people with no imagination to take them to places they didn't really know they wanted to go to in the first place where they can be bored silly, eat their own body weight in unhealthy food and then go home and watch *Taggart*. If I ever turn out like that,' he said, turning to Gabriel, 'you will shoot me, won't you? If I ever watch *Taggart*, just put me out of my misery there and then.'

'It's a promise,' said Gabriel solemnly.

'Well, I thought it would be good for us all to do something together,' said Braindead. 'Seeing as we haven't really managed it so far.'

'It's a great idea, Braindead,' said Katy. 'Ignore Daniel, he's just a miserable old goat.'

'He shouldn't be,' said Braindead. 'He did get to use the honeymoon suite again last night, after all.'

'Some use that was,' huffed Daniel.

'What?' said Katy. 'Don't tell me you missed out again! You had hours to make use of that room. Gabriel didn't collect Silvie from our room until after ten!'

'Well,' said Daniel. He looked at a loss. 'We were just tired. We went out for a meal then rushed back to the suite but I fell asleep. Having been out until late the night before, I just didn't have the energy. A few Martinis and I was out for the count.'

'Out late two nights running,' scoffed Braindead. 'Now who sounds old? You sound like you need to go on a day trip and then watch some *Taggart*.'

'Look, it's no big deal,' said Daniel. 'When you have a baby, everyone knows that sleep is the priority, right? Then the baby grows a bit and you get your verve back. That's just normal, right?'

'We shall see, shall we?' said Katy. 'Our turn tonight. Are you still okay to look after Millie and Jack for a couple of hours?' she asked Daniel.

'Sure,' he replied. 'You planning on *using* the room or going out for a meal? Now there's a dilemma for you. Would you rather do it in the honeymoon suite or have a steak and a cocktail?'

'That is an impossible question to answer,' said Katy, holding her head on one side. 'I mean, I don't know what I'll be in the mood for, come 5 p.m.'

'Exactly,' said Daniel. 'I never realised that having children takes all the spontaneity out of it. Opportunities now need to be spotted from a mile off and strategically planned. That is not what it's all about, is it? Talk about the opposite of foreplay: "Can you do a week next Wednesday because Silvie has a play date?"'

'Anyway, speaking of well-planned evenings out, how did it go with Ollie last night?' Gabriel asked Braindead. 'I hope you didn't mind me prioritising my husband.'

Daniel gasped. 'I actually think hearing him say that is better than you know what,' he said, looking slightly flushed.

'Well,' said Braindead. 'We found a great bar to watch the golf in.'

'What?' said Daniel. 'I thought you were off out to find him a lady friend?'

'We did attempt to after that but it turns out he can't chat up women to save his life, he can't dance and he's a mournful singer.'

'I should have come with you, shouldn't I?' said Daniel, shaking his head.

'You were supposed to be having sex!' exclaimed Katy.

'I know, but if there's anyone who should be teaching the poor lad how to talk to women it should be me. I am, after all, the master of it.'

'Really, it's such a waste you're gay, isn't it?' commented Katy.

'It really is,' said Daniel.

'Look, the coach is here now,' said Braindead. 'Are we all ready for a grand day out?'

'Yeah,' said Logan jumping up and down in excitement next to his dad. Nobody else joined in.

*

It took approximately twenty minutes to get them on the coach as Daniel insisted on having an argument with the tour guide. Apparently you weren't supposed to take pushchairs on the coach, but Daniel was insisting that theirs came with them. A stand-up row commenced with the two of them standing nose to nose until Gabriel intervened in Spanish and somehow managed to convince the tour guide that the pushchair should go in the boot of the coach and they should get on their way.

The entire coach gave a sigh of relief as they pulled away and clapped Gabriel on his way back to his seat as he sat down shyly.

'What did you say to her?' Daniel hissed at his husband.

'I said she had beautiful eyes and that you were intimidated by her. You needed to show her you were powerful because you have a complex about your masculinity so in the interests of not delaying the rest of the passengers, would she allow me to put the pushchair in the boot of the coach and get you to sit down? I also asked her who her optician was as I liked her glasses.'

'I'm not sure I'm pleased about any of your tactics,' said Daniel huffily.

'We are on our way and the pushchair is with us. I would say my tactics have been most successful.'

'Attention, please,' said the guide, tapping into a microphone. 'Apologies for the slight delay,' she continued, staring at Daniel. 'We now have an approximately fifty-five-minute journey to our destination.'

'Fifty-five minutes!' exclaimed Daniel. 'I could walk there quicker. I mean, it's only just around the bay, isn't it? Didn't they say it was fifteen minutes away when we booked it?'

Gabriel asked the lady a question in Spanish.

'She says we have to make four stops at other hotels until we get to the private beach,' he said. 'That's why it takes so long.'

'Oh my God!' exclaimed Daniel. 'This is already a nightmare.'

The woman at the front of the coach threw another comment at Gabriel in Spanish.

Gabriel smiled but he did not translate.

'What did she say?' asked Daniel.

'That you are a very rude Englishman and she wonders why I tolerate you.'

'Did you tell her it was due to my charm and good nature and great looks?' said Daniel, raising his eyebrows.

'No, I said it was because you had an enormous… apartment and I married you for your money.'

'I'll take that,' said Daniel. 'She's only jealous. I mean, what kind of man is she ever going to attract? Is that a moustache?'

Again, Gabriel did a translation. The lady smiled and blew Daniel a kiss.

'I told her that when you meet women like her you wish you were straight.'

'Hmmm,' said Daniel, turning to face the window. 'In her dreams.'

*

Abby, Daniel and Ben looked green by the time they got off the coach at the 'enchanting beachfront location'. The road down to the seafront had been long and winding and noisy as all the babies on board decided to kick off at the same time.

'Seriously?' said Daniel, staggering off. 'I have never felt so sick in all of my life. I don't think I can even hold Silvie.'

'Here, give her to me,' said Gabriel, coming up behind him. 'I'll have her.'

'You will make someone a wonderful husband one day, you know,' said Daniel, handing her over. He collapsed onto the floor and held his head in his hands.

'Okay, everyone,' said the tour guide, striding past Daniel and standing in front of the dispirited crowd that had alighted from the bus and gathered on the tarmac of the car park. 'We have a short walk to our exclusive beach where drinks are waiting for us and some very special local entertainment. Please follow me.'

Daniel groaned again. 'I'm not sure I can move,' he said.

The tour guide rippled out a flash of Spanish directed at Gabriel.

'She says that you look so pale, like a vampire,' translated Gabriel.

'Vampire!' said Daniel, looking up sharply at the tour guide but it was too late, she had turned her back and was starting to lead the group away. 'Did she really say that or are you winding me up now?' he asked.

'No, she really said that,' smiled Gabriel. 'I think she doesn't believe we are together. She thinks I must be joking that I married you and so she is enjoying this pulling apart of the pathetic Englishman in front of his face in a foreign language.'

'You haven't defended me?'

Gabriel shook his head, laughing. 'This is much funnier,' he said.

'But she thinks you are in on the joke?'

'Uh huh,' said Gabriel. 'What a blessing to understand how you come across in a foreign country,' he told him. 'What great learning you can get from that.' He turned his back and started to follow the rest of the crowd.

'My husband...' Daniel began. 'My husband is... is...'

'Is doing an utterly sterling job of showing you that you need to be more considerate of other people,' said Katy. 'And to get down off your high horse sometimes and just be... just be like everyone else instead of thinking you constantly deserve better than everyone else.'

Daniel stared at her with his mouth open.

'Come on,' she continued, holding her hand out to him. 'We'll miss our free drink if we don't catch up with them soon.'

*

Katy dared not look at Daniel when they arrived on the 'exclusive beach'. Exclusive as a description was stretching it to say the least. They were clearly sharing their 'exclusive' experience with several other parties who had already arrived. Strips of the beach were separated by rows of upturned sun loungers forming temporary barriers to make sure no-one strayed. The worst thing was that whilst their strip was completely barren with only litter as decoration, the strip next to them had trestle tables covered with pristine white tablecloths and laden with pastries and cookies and coffee and cocktails. Guests lazed on sun loungers under blue and white parasols as a clown gathered the children under a gazebo and proceeded to make animals out of balloons, keeping them all enraptured and out of their parents' hair.

Katy glanced at Daniel as they all hobbled onto the sand struggling with nappy bags and towels and beach toys as well as the essential sun cream, wet wipes, random children's snacks and bottles of water. They dumped everything into a pile on the dusty sand and peered out to the cloudy sky as a plastic carrier bag whisked its untidy way across the shoreline. No-one said a word. All that could be heard were the shrieks of delight from the children next door as they went into battle with balloon-shaped swords.

Katy looked along their stretch of beach. Not a trestle table in sight, not a drink, not a snack, not a sun lounger, not a parasol and certainly not a hint of a clown. There was absolutely nothing to show for the euros they'd doled out on the promise of an exclusive all-you-can-eat and-drink beach barbeque with Spain's finest local entertainment. There was just sand, litter and a much better party going on right next door. It couldn't possibly be any worse.

*

'Shall I go and find these free cocktails then?' said Braindead brightly. Even he looked somewhat disappointed by the reality of his much-anticipated day trip.

It must have been a half-hour later when he arrived back with a tray of plastic glasses with a red liquid splashed into them.

He solemnly passed them round.

Daniel looked at him, then looked at Gabriel, who was too distracted by Silvie to take any notice. He took a sip. It was of the cheap sangria nature. The kind you buy in the supermarket alongside the cheap orange and apple juice. It tasted of sour grapes. It certainly didn't taste like there was enough alcohol in it to dislodge the growing feeling that this trip had been a massive mistake.

Katy blew her cheeks out and sighed at the thought of being stranded here for at least four hours with the wind whipping sand into their faces, the clouds covering the sun and the alcohol that didn't contain alcohol. The day suddenly stretched infinitely in front of her.

'Is everyone okay?' came a voice from behind them as the tour guide walked over.

No-one spoke for a moment. They all exchanged glances, knowing what was slowly dawning on them. That this was going to be a colossal waste of time and money and that little joy could come from this situation. That the marketing of the grand day out far exceeded the reality. They were trapped.

They should be honest. They should complain. But they couldn't complain because it had been Braindead's idea. Poor Braindead, who was having the worst holiday of all as his wife did her best to have a separate holiday entirely. If they complained, he would feel like it was his fault and no-one wanted to put him through that.

Katy glanced over at Daniel, who could have been their saving grace. The one who would have the arrogance to put this terrible situation right, but she had just shot him down. Literally told him that reacting to this situation would be further proof of what an arrogant tosser he could be.

But worst of all: the biggest factor preventing them from complaining was of course the fact that they were British. Rendered polite and un-confrontational in the face of bad service, and therefore when the tour guide asked again if they were all okay, they all chorused back with a cheerful if non-committal, 'Yes, fine.'

No-one uttered a word as she walked away.

Katy downed her drink, her fingers now sticky and clumped with sand. She needed to wash them in the sea but the sea looked dark and brooding on this cloudy day.

'Can I go and see the clown?' asked Millie.

Katy's heart sank. She had been waiting for this.

'No, I'm afraid not,' said Katy.

'Why not?' asked Millie.

'Because the clown is part of that party and not ours,' replied Katy.

'Are we at a party?' asked Millie. 'It doesn't look like a party. Why can't we go to the party with the clown?'

'Because we can't,' said Katy, looking nervously over at Braindead, not wanting to upset him.

'Why not?'

'Because we didn't pay to go to that party.'

'You have to pay to go to a party?' asked Millie.

'Yes,' said Katy, wishing her daughter would shut up.

'Did we pay for this party?' asked Millie, looking round the barren beach at the other miserable people wishing they were somewhere else.

'Yes,' replied Katy.

'Why didn't we pay to go to the party with the clown?' asked Millie.

'Because we just didn't,' said Katy, wishing the sand would swallow her up.

'Shall we build a sandcastle?' said Braindead suddenly, a look of panic on his face that his treasured day was not going to plan.

Katy thought her heart would break for him. Abby was already stretched out on a towel applying suntan lotion. Ignoring the distress of her husband.

'Yes!' said Katy enthusiastically, leaping up. Anything to get her out of the conversation she was currently in with her daughter. 'Why don't we have a competition? See who can build the best sandcastle.'

'I will win,' said Gabriel. 'I am an architect after all.'

'Bollocks,' said Ben, also getting up. 'I won a sandcastle-building competition at Butlin's when I was seven. I have form.'

'I shall direct,' announced Daniel, holding Silvie. 'Who wants me to be the creative director on their team? I am award-winning.'

'Me,' said Braindead straight away. 'You can tell me and Logan what to do, can't he, buddy?'

'Yes,' nodded Logan. 'I'll dig and dig and dig and dig and dig and dig.'

'Okay, buddy,' said Braindead. 'Abby, are you coming on our team?'

'No, I'll sit this out,' she said, getting her phone out and starting to scroll through as she placed her sunglasses on her head.

'You sure?'

'Yep,' she nodded.

And so the morning was somewhat redeemed as they dug. The sand proved to be excellent and made fantastic sculptures once water was added. Katy looked up at one point to see Daniel happily making pillars of sand to adorn the sandcastles that Braindead and Logan had constructed. Millie had joined Gabriel's team and they were talking gently to each other, debating and agreeing where each castle should go and which shells should adorn them. Ben was having the time of his life digging as deep as he could go with Jack at his side, caked in sand, as Katy built castles behind them, enjoying the mind-numbing productivity of the task. Only Abby remained alone, unconvinced that the activity was worthwhile or enjoyable. The rest of the adults sat with their backs to their neighbours trying to ignore any signs of their enjoyment.

*

They were all in a dramatically better mood when lunch was called. At twelve thirty they wandered up to a wide concrete terrace where picnic tables had appeared. They had been billed as being laden with *'All-you-can-eat traditional meats cooked on an open fire accompanied by a vast array of salads and side dishes.'*

There was a mound of what looked like charcoal but which must have been the traditional meats, along with some anaemic-looking frankfurters for the kids, a couple of green salads and a dubious-looking mound of pasta.

Acceptance set in that this was the level of the 'superior and exclusive beach barbeque' as they collected their plates and sighed and picked their way into the charcoal to actually try and find some meat, then trudged over to sit at the benches under the trees nearby.

'I might go vegetarian,' said Ben, picking at his unidentifiable food.

'Seriously?' asked Katy.

'For this meal,' he replied.

'You should have done what I did and had a kids' hotdog,' she said. 'Not bad at all. You can't go wrong with hotdog, can you?'

'You are a genius,' said Ben, leaping up. 'I knew there was reason why I married you.'

'Bring as many as you can carry,' she shouted after him.

'You enjoy?' said the tour rep coming round as the half-full plates began to be taken away. 'You must be full, yes?'

Daniel looked at Gabriel. The tension was back. He was bursting to complain but couldn't bear to behave in the way that Gabriel had predicted.

'It's been delightful,' said Daniel to the tour rep. He was rewarded with a warm smile from her and a smirk from Gabriel.

Then Gabriel addressed the woman and soon her warm smile began to fade. His words came out swiftly and quietly in his lilting Spanish. Every so often he shrugged and cast his hands around him and every time she tried to respond he held his hand up to silence her. When he finally came to the end he fell silent and she also fell silent, her mouth open.

'Now,' he suddenly barked. She scurried off, calling the waiters to her as she went.

'What did you say?' asked Katy in awe.

'I spoke the truth,' he replied grimly.

'About what?'

'About this.' Again he cast his hand around. He looked deadly serious. A look that few of them had seen before.

'I told her that I was ashamed that this is what my country considers to be a special meal and a special beach. That it upset me that they had let me down so. And that you are not full, the food is just foul.'

'I have never fancied you more,' announced Daniel, touching his arm.

'Me neither,' muttered Katy.

Suddenly the tour guide reappeared, placing two bottles of wine and some glasses on the table in front of them, before scurrying off again.

'I fancy you as well now,' said Ben, leaning forward to pour the wine.

The next minute the waiters produced ice creams for all the children along with packets of crisps and more hotdogs for the grown-ups.

Gabriel shouted the tour rep over once more.

'For everyone,' he said, indicating the rest of the guests gaping at them and their now laden table.

A look of horror flashed over the woman's face before she scurried off. Before long each table was furnished with wine and snacks and ice cream to compensate for the woeful offering so far.

*

And then the sun came out and the clouds drifted away and out came the lunch entertainment just as they were half way down their second bottle of wine. A lone guitarist sauntered up and sat down under an olive tree. He raised the instrument to his knee and struck a chord before the most marvellous music tumbled forth. It really was quite breathtaking and, for the first time that day, it exceeded all of their expectations. They sat in awe as he strummed his way through some magical bars until Millie went up to her mother and whispered in her ear: 'I want to dance, Mummy.'

'Off you go then,' she replied.

'Come with me.'

Katy hadn't had nearly enough wine to dance in the middle of the day to a lone guitarist in front of a bunch of strangers.

'Ask your dad,' she whispered.

Millie trundled round to the other side of the table and whispered in Ben's ear. Katy watched as he looked over at her, horrified. He shook his head at Millie.

'Please,' Katy heard her whine. 'Please, Daddy.'

He shook his head again.

He whispered in her ear and Katy watched as Millie glanced at her mum and then shook her head at her dad, no doubt explaining that she had also refused.

'*Senorita*,' said Gabriel, holding his hand out to his sandcastle-building partner. 'Would you dance with me?'

Millie jumped up and down excitedly and ran into his arms. He held her up and proceeded to waltz around in front of the guitarist, much to Millie's delight.

'How come you get to marry the Dad of the Century?' Katy asked Daniel. 'It's not like you deserve him or anything.'

'I must have generated some seriously good karma, mustn't I?' said Daniel, stroking Silvie's head. 'And to be honest, I don't think I deserve him either. He is rather perfect, isn't he?'

'Come up,' Gabriel declared to Braindead and Abby. 'You must join us. It would be rude not to.'

'I need to watch Logan,' said Braindead, shaking his head.

'I can watch him,' offered Katy. He was sitting at their feet, still digging.

'No,' said Braindead. 'No, it's fine.'

'Come on,' urged Abby. 'Don't be such an old fuddy-duddy. Come and dance with me?'

'No,' said Braindead, shaking his head vigorously. 'I need to watch Logan.'

'But Katy can watch him,' protested Abby. 'She just said. Come on, just for a minute. Come and dance with me.'

Braindead stood firm. 'I'm happier playing with our son,' he said.

Abby paused for a moment, looking at him.

'I can see that,' she said sharply. 'Maybe it would be nice if for once you decided you wanted to play with me instead.'

She turned her back and moved towards Gabriel and Millie. She began to throw some flamboyant flamenco-style moves. It wasn't long before she was joined by some of the other holidaymakers as well as attracting some admiring glances from the men who lined the makeshift dance floor, sipping on their wine.

'Go and dance with Abby,' Katy urged Braindead.

'She's fine,' he said, shaking his head. 'We're all right here, aren't we, buddy,' he said, smiling down at his son and ignoring the attention that Abby was gathering.

*

In the end, they were all quite disappointed to be told that it was time to leave. The guitarist had played for a good hour and Gabriel had ensured that the wine had kept flowing, which had led to a most unlikely enjoyable lunch. They all trooped back up to the car park feeling more contented than expected.

'Oh brilliant!' Abby shrieked as they began to climb aboard the coach. She was staring at her phone in a state of utter excitement. 'We can go!' she said, a broad smile spreading over her face.

'Go where?' asked Braindead.

'Rachel just texted to say that they've managed to get us tickets to join them on the party boat tonight,' she said. 'They said it was sold out but they got Ruth on it and she's managed to wangle it. We can go!'

'A party boat?' questioned Braindead.

'Yeah,' she said, looking down at her phone again.

'I thought we were all going to go to that steak restaurant tonight,' he said.

'Well, you can still go,' she said to them. She looked up and finally noticed the crestfallen look on her husband's face.

'I'll stay in tomorrow night,' she gasped. 'You go out with Ben again tomorrow. Do whatever you like.'

Braindead said nothing, his mouth hanging open.

'Ruth has jumped through hoops to get us these tickets,' said Abby. 'Rather than sitting by the pool all day apparently she's been on the phone trying to get it sorted. We can't let her down now and anyway it's part of Cassie's hen do. We have to go.'

'Cassie who you met just a few days ago,' said Braindead. 'Who you will probably never see again in your life after this week.'

'Oh, we are invited to the wedding. For sure. She just has to check when she gets back if they can get us into the reception but we are going. She really wants us there. Fi said so. So you see, I can't not go tonight, not when she has invited us to her wedding.'

No-one was looking at Abby and Braindead. The others all busied themselves with nappy bags or pretended to struggle with getting small children to sit down.

'But we've hardly spent any time together,' said Braindead. 'This holiday was supposed to be about the three of us. About enjoying our first proper holiday with Logan and we've hardly seen you.'

There was a pause.

'But what about me?' Abby eventually said. 'It's always about the three of us. Always. All the time! What about me?' There was a hint of defiance in her voice.

'You can have fun with me and Logan,' said Braindead. 'We can all have fun together?'

Silence again.

'You don't understand,' she said. 'You're not me. I'm going tonight whether you like it or not.'

Chapter Eighteen

No-one said much on the bus home. No-one knew what to say. Even the tour rep was quiet, no doubt thinking about how she was going to explain the bottles of wine and the snacks that had been given away on the trip.

Seeing her sitting at the front of the bus looking dejected, Gabriel got up from his seat and sat down next to her, talking gently in Spanish. Eventually she hugged him and he rejoined the group.

'What did you say to her?' asked Daniel. 'Have you told her to apologise to me?'

'No,' said Gabriel, shaking his head. 'I asked for her boss's email address and promised that I will write to him to explain why he won't be making a profit on today's trip and that the fault does not lie with her. I will also tell him that I will spread the word about his company in the big bad world of British social media unless he stops ripping tourists off. And I shall be sending my father to check on him in a month to make sure.'

He settled back in his seat looking grim, before thanking Braindead for organising the day and saying that he hoped that it had not been too spoiled by his fellow countrymen.

'You saved the day, mate,' mumbled Braindead.

'No, you did,' said Gabriel, putting his hand on his shoulder. 'My memory of the beautiful creation I made with Millie in the sand this morning will be treasured forever. That would not have happened without you.'

'At least it's our turn for the honeymoon suite,' Katy whispered to Ben on the seat behind them.

'Great,' he replied, his eyes lighting up. 'We'll get back and move our stuff straight away shall we?'

'Good idea,' replied Katy. She reached into her bag for her phone, having heard it ping. She should have ignored it. In fact she should have left her phone at home. What could possibly be so important that she had to answer it now?

Hi – it's Cassie. I hear Abby is coming tonight. Please will you come too. We have two more tickets – please. X

'Who's that?' asked Ben.

Katy let out a big sigh. 'It's Cassie,' she said. 'The bride-to-be. She wants me to go on the party boat tonight too.'

'No,' said Ben immediately. 'No way! Daniel and Gabriel are all poised to babysit. We have a night planned. Like, a proper holiday night. Like a night that normal people have on holiday.'

'You mean food, drink and sex?' muttered Katy.

'That's exactly what I mean. You can't back out of that now.'

Katy read the text again. 'She sounds like she really wants me to go,' she said. 'I'm a bit worried about her, actually. When we went out last time, she kind of said she didn't really want to get married. She's got cold feet. Actually she's got frozen feet.'

'So?' said Ben, getting agitated. 'Why is that your problem? Where are all the other hens whilst she's having this crisis?'

'Just happy to be getting pissed on a hen do,' replied Katy. 'I get the impression that the future happiness of the bride-to-be is kind of irrelevant.'

'Brutal!' exclaimed Ben.

'Maybe,' pondered Katy.

'Christ, it's hard being a girl, isn't it?' said Ben.

'Do you know what, it is,' agreed Katy.

'Please come out with me tonight,' he said, giving her his best puppy-dog eyes.

She laughed and put her phone back in her bag. Text unanswered. 'There is no place I'd rather be,' she said.

*

Katy couldn't help but run around the honeymoon suite in a state of joy once they had transferred all of their stuff.

'Where shall we go tonight then?' she asked Ben, coming to an abrupt halt and giving him a peck on the cheek.

'Well, Daniel and Gabriel say they can cope for maybe three hours so why don't we nip out for a quick one – as in meal, at the place on the corner that you have been lusting over – and then come back here for a quick one. If you see what I mean.'

'You are so naughty,' she giggled. 'But it sounds like a cunning plan if ever I heard one. We can't waste all this, can we? I mean, it is the honeymoon suite after all.'

'Absolutely!' declared Ben. 'Someone *has* to have sex in it. I mean, it's probably mandatory and obviously Ollie didn't manage it and Daniel and Gabriel were thwarted so it is our absolute duty.'

'To Queen and Country,' said Katy.

'To Queen and Country,' agreed Ben.

They both crashed onto the bed, thinking they might just have time for a quick nap whilst the kids watched the telly, when there came a rap at the door.

'Do you think we get complimentary room service up here?' said Katy excitedly.

Unfortunately when she answered the door it was a forlorn-looking Braindead standing there rather than a waiter with a trolley of goodies.

'Come in,' she said. 'Kids are just watching the TV and we were just planning our night out.'

'Will you go with Abby?' Braindead asked before she could say anything else. 'Hi Ben,' he muttered.

'Hello mate, what can we do for you?'

'I came to ask if Katy would go with Abby on this party cruise thing.'

'Aw, come on, mate,' said Ben. 'We were just planning our night out, you know, without the kids and with access to the honeymoon suite.'

Braindead blinked back at him.

'I'm worried about her on her own. She's not herself,' he said, shaking his head. 'She needs someone to keep an eye on her.'

Katy sat down hard on the bed.

'She's a grown woman,' said Ben.

'I know,' said Braindead. He looked up, his eyes all watery. 'But she doesn't seem to be thinking straight. I just want someone there to keep her safe, that's all.'

Braindead looked on the brink of collapse.

Katy looked at Ben. He shrugged, resigned.

'I'll go,' said Katy. 'But I can't promise that I will be able to bring her home or anything like that. All I can do is be a...'

'A presence,' said Braindead.

'Precisely,' agreed Katy. 'That's all I can do.'

'Do you think Daniel will go again too?' asked Braindead. 'To keep you company?'

'No way,' replied Katy. 'He said he's not touching a hen party for the rest of his life.'

'Oh,' said Braindead, looking sad. 'I'm so sorry. You're really not going to enjoy it, are you?'

'I know who should go with you,' interjected Ben.

'Gabriel?' suggested Katy. 'Good God, they would eat him alive!'

'What about Ollie?' said Ben.

'Ollie?' said Katy. 'You want me to take Ollie with me?'

'Hen party... perfect for him, don't you think, women desperate for... well, for something. And he needs help, believe me he needs the forwardness of a hen party to bring him out of himself, he is *petrified* of women.'

'He's petrified of women and you want me to put him in amongst that bunch of lunatics?' said Katy.

'Look, it can't do him any harm. It'll get him out, with women, on a night that doesn't matter. No pressure. Could do him the world of good. And it repays him for lending us the honeymoon suite. Everyone's happy.'

'So you're sending me on a night out to babysit a much younger man that I barely know who is socially awkward the minute he gets in front of a single female, and a wife and mother who is having some kind of midlife crisis? And to top it all I am doing this instead of being taken out for a meal by my husband and having sex on my holiday.'

Ben and Braindead said nothing.

'Is that what it is?' Braindead asked eventually. 'A midlife crisis? Abby's a bit young for that, isn't she?'

Katy slumped. He looked so miserable.

'I don't know,' she admitted. 'But something's not right, is it? I certainly think that she is having a tough time coping with how much her life has changed in the last couple of years.'

'But it has all changed for the better. We got married, we had Logan, they're both good things.'

'They are but you do lose some things too. You lose freedom and Abby stopped working for a while and that's tough. You feel like you've lost your identity. It's a massive readjustment.'

'Have I ruined her?' asked Braindead, swallowing. 'Have I made her life terrible?'

'No!' said Katy and Ben together.

'It's not your fault,' added Katy. 'These things just happen.'

'What do I do?' Braindead asked.

'Talk to her. Get her to talk.'

He said nothing. He looked as though he might cry. All that could be heard was the dubbed cartoon droning on in the background.

He turned to go, his shoulders slumped.

'You will go though, won't you?' he asked, turning round just before he left the room.

'Of course I will,' said Katy.

He shuffled out and shut the door behind him.

'Poor Braindead,' she muttered.

'Poor me!' exclaimed Ben, flinging himself on the bed. 'I'm never going to have sex on this holiday, am I?'

Chapter Nineteen

'Why am I doing this?' said Katy as she sat in a chair at the bar, bouncing Jack up and down on her knee as she waited patiently for her two unlikely evening companions to appear.

'You're doing it for Braindead,' said Ben. 'I think.'

'And what about Ollie? A young man I barely know forced out on a night out with me and a group of crazy hen party women. How has my holiday ended up this way? When I get home and people ask me if I had a nice holiday, I will say: "Actually, I wasn't on a family holiday, I went on a hen do with a load of strangers and then tried to fix up another complete stranger whose fiancée had jilted him at the altar. That was my holiday!"'

'There will be other holidays,' sighed Ben.

'You think?' she said, nodding at their two children. 'You think we will get a normal civilised holiday within the next ten years with this pair around? We're destined for a decade with a complete lack of relaxation or respite, you know that, don't you?'

'Can't wait,' he smiled, reaching out and clutching her hand. 'Here we go,' he said, nodding towards the door. 'Here comes your date for the evening.'

She looked up to see an unusual little party if ever there was one coming towards them across the bar. Daniel, Gabriel and Silvie escorting

Ollie, who was looking actually pretty sharp although he didn't look very happy about the prospect of his evening.

'Looking good, man,' said Ben.

'I'm not sure about this,' said Ollie.

'What part aren't you sure about?' asked Ben. 'Spending the evening with my wife or the prospect of half a dozen hungry hens ready to rip you limb from limb?'

Ollie went pale.

'None of it,' he whimpered.

'My wife's not that bad, is she?' asked Ben.

'No, no, she's lovely. I mean, she's a very nice lady, not pretty or anything…'

'Oh thanks,' muttered Katy.

'No, you are pretty,' he protested, looking warily at Ben. 'You know, for your age, if you were single… I don't know what I mean.'

'You don't fancy me,' said Katy. 'Is that what you mean?'

'Of course not,' said Ollie, 'I would never…'

'She's just winding you up,' interrupted Ben. 'Ignore her. She's really looking forward to taking you out.'

Katy raised her eyebrows.

'Now do you like his makeover?' asked Daniel.

Katy screwed up her eyes and scrutinised Ollie. She knew he looked different somehow.

'What have you done to him?' she asked.

'I did a *Queer Eye*!' said Daniel excitedly. 'I have literally always wanted to do one and the minute I heard that he was coming with you on the hen do, well, it was such an opportunity, despite the fact I practically had to drag him kicking and screaming to our room.'

'Well, he has been in a room naked with you once already this holiday,' said Ben, 'so I can understand the reluctance. But what's doing a *Queer Eye*?'

'Have you never seen *Queer Eye for the Straight Guy*?' asked Daniel incredulously. 'It's an American TV show where five gay guys get to do a makeover on a straight guy and turn his life around.'

'They turn him gay?' asked Ben, confused.

'No!' said Daniel. 'As if. No, they sort out his clothes and his skincare regime and his diet and his interior decoration and typically shave a lot of hair off him, although unfortunately Ollie didn't have too much hair to begin with so I couldn't transform him in quite the way they do.'

'Skincare regime?' questioned Ben.

'Oh yes,' said Daniel.

'So they turn him gay?'

'No!'

'I'm just winding you up,' said Ben, punching him on the arm. 'But seriously, Ollie, if you feel you have been violated at all by the application of cleanser and moisturiser, I'm sure I could find you a charity phone line that could help.'

Ollie just looked in shock and didn't answer.

'You look great,' Katy told him. 'Really great. You did a good job, Daniel. Ignore Ben.'

'Do you like my green linen shirt on him? See how it brings out the subtle highlights in his hair,' continued Daniel.

'Subtle green highlights?' asked Ben.

'It's all to do with tone,' said Daniel, brushing him off. 'We've also had a really good chat about how to deal with these women he's going to meet tonight.'

Finally Ollie spoke. 'Apparently I should act shy,' he said in wonder.

'Don't you agree?' said Daniel. 'Acting shy and mysterious will drive them wild. This crowd will be all over him and when he tells them he was jilted at the altar... well... he'll have them eating out of his hand.'

'I don't want them eating out of my hand,' protested Ollie. 'Is that what they do on hen nights? Eat out of your hand? But I never use hand sanitiser, I don't like how it makes your skin feel.'

They all stared at him in silence and for the first time Katy noticed he was shaking slightly with nerves.

'He didn't mean literally eating out of your hand,' she said. 'Now I want you to ignore everything that Daniel has told you. All you need to be is yourself. Please. Please don't try to be anything but.'

He nodded at her but still he was shaking.

A clatter at the door heralded the arrival of Braindead, Abby and Logan. Braindead was carrying Logan on his hip and wearing a grim look on his face. Abby had more make-up on than the woman with the worst skin on the make-up counter at Boots. She was also wearing a very short skirt and a bikini top with a cropped macramé cardigan over her shoulders and very high heels.

'Shall we go?' she said to Katy. 'The boat will leave without us if we don't get there by half past.'

'Yes, of course,' said Katy, trying to not stare at Abby's boobs spilling over her bikini top. She'd put her swimsuit on under her skirt and top but had really no intention of taking anything off. She'd been tempted to put a book in her bag as she had some kind of notion that she might be able to hide herself away in a quiet corner. But Ben had laughed heartily and she knew she was being ridiculous. Instead she'd thrown in a small towel and a bottle of water. Maybe equally ridiculous.

Chapter Twenty

Two hours later, Katy sat Ollie down on a seat below deck on the party boat and told him to breathe. He was hyperventilating, such was his distress. What had they done to him? He might never speak to another woman again. Katy wondered whether she should dial 999 before she remembered they were not in the UK. She wondered if she should call the lifeguard. What emergency services did you summon aboard a boat? She had no idea. Of course she should be able to summon a tour rep, but from what she had seen upstairs there were no reps responsible enough to help her. The last one she had seen had jumped into the water then removed his trunks and waved them over his head triumphantly. Not the kind of man you needed in a crisis. She'd call Ben. He'd perhaps know what to do with a traumatised, hyperventilating young man who had been led into a situation entirely against his own free will and was now suffering because of it. She could go to jail, she thought miserably. What had they been thinking?

*

It had all started relatively innocently. Katy, Abby and Ollie had arrived at the harbour and were soon spotted by the hen party.

'Hey, Abby, over here,' shouted Rachel. Katy looked over. They were all relatively sanely dressed in matching pink T-shirts and various types of sarongs, oh, and penis-shaped deely-boppers that Katy tried to ignore.

Cassie dashed over to Katy and enveloped her in a massive hug.

'I didn't think you were coming,' she gasped.

'I'm sorry,' replied Katy. 'I forgot to text you back.'

'Doesn't matter,' said Cassie. 'You're here now. Just so you know, Ruth has planned some games but I don't want to do them.' Cassie was looking slightly manic.

'Right,' said Katy. 'Well, don't then.'

'Yes,' said Cassie. 'You're right, I won't. Not if I don't want to.'

'Of course,' said Katy. 'It's your hen party, you don't have to do anything.'

Cassie nodded furiously. 'Of course you're right. When Ruth tries to make me do it, you will stick up for me, won't you?'

'Er, well, if you need me to,' replied Katy.

'Where's Daniel?' asked Ruth, interrupting.

'Oh, he's having some time with his husband and daughter,' said Katy, 'So we brought along a friend we have made at the resort. Hope that's all right? This is Ollie.'

Katy looked at Ollie, who was looking absolutely terrified at the sight of a sea of glittery penises bobbing around at eye level.

'Pleased to meet you,' he mumbled.

'Single?' barked Bridget, eyeing him up and down.

'Er, yes, actually I am,' he said, looking at the floor.

'Weh hey, girls,' said Fi, shoving her fist in the air. 'We've got a live one. I thought we'd got it made, getting a gay guy to tag along but a single guy... my God, this is like a dream come true. I tell you what,

Ruth,' she added. 'Us meeting Abby on the plane has been the best bit of planning you have ever achieved.'

Ruth grinned and handed a T-shirt to Abby, one to Katy and then one to Ollie.

'I don't have to wear this, do I?' he said to Katy, his eyes as wide as saucers.

'If you want to be in our gang,' said Fi, 'you have to wear the T-shirt.'

'But, it might not fit?' he whimpered.

'They're all large, don't worry. We chose the size based on the size of Bridget's tits. It was cheaper if they were all the same size apparently, wasn't it, Ruth?'

How Katy stopped herself from looking at Bridget's chest she had no idea.

'But Daniel lent me his shirt especially,' continued Ollie.

'He won't mind,' said Fi. 'He'd be totally up for wearing a pink T-shirt with "Mother of the Bride" on the back.'

'What!' he exclaimed. Katy watched as he unravelled the T-shirt to find that indeed it said 'Mother of the Bride' on the back.

'My mum was supposed to be coming but she got a slot to get liposuction and so she decided that would be better for her – you know, for the sake of the photos and that – and so she cancelled,' said Cassie.

Katy gave Cassie a sympathetic smile. Boy, there was some pressure to get married if your mother was having liposuction just for the photos. Maybe she should have another chat with Cassie later to see how she was feeling about her forthcoming marriage. Perhaps then the evening would not be completely wasted.

'You want me to get on that boat in a pink T-shirt with "Mother of the Bride" on it?' asked Ollie, now quite pale. He gave Katy a look that nearly broke her heart.

'Come on, it will get you in the spirit,' said Bridget as they all crowded round him expectantly. 'We'll stand round you whilst you change, if you like, so no-one can see you.'

Ollie looked at Katy in astonishment and then slowly began to unbutton his shirt. Katy felt her whole body clench. She knew it was coming, she could feel it. She wanted to stop it, but she didn't know how.

'Da, da dar, de da da dar…' began Rachel with a smirk as she hummed the unmistakable tune to 'The Stripper'. Soon everyone had joined in and Katy could feel the heat from Ollie's cheeks.

This was a huge mistake, she thought, not for the first or the last time that evening.

*

They stood in line waiting to get onto the party boat. Ollie didn't look or speak to Katy whilst Abby took swigs of vodka from a bottle that Rachel was passing around.

They got on the boat and headed for the bar. It was of course absolutely rammed but Ruth managed to push her way to the front and came back with as many cocktails as she could carry, as well as two bottles of lager which she had stashed in her bag and handed over to Ollie.

'There you go,' she said. 'This will help.'

He smiled at her gratefully and practically downed a bottle in one.

They all pushed their way up the stairs and onto the top deck where a DJ was banging out pulsating rhythms, the dance floor already crammed with a mass of semi-naked twenty-something bodies. Firm flesh swam in front of Katy's face. Flesh that hadn't been ravaged by childbirth or years of eating too much sugar and too much fat. Flesh that was perfect and smooth and lacking in any cellulite or stretch marks or unwanted hair. This was fast becoming Katy's worst nightmare as well as Ollie's. There was no way she would be donning her swimsuit here. Her demure swimsuit that still didn't cover enough of her dimply legs and fast-emerging bingo wings. She swallowed and looked for Abby. As she took a swig of her drink she spotted her. Right in the middle of the heaving dancers in her bikini, her eyes closed, a smile on her face. She wasn't sure this hedonistic atmosphere was going to do much for Abby's state of mind either.

She felt someone nudge her arm and she turned around in utter fear, hoping it wasn't one of the topless men strutting about with waxy smooth chests, oily from sunscreen, who were making her feel quite queasy.

But it wasn't. It was Ollie holding out four shot glasses.

'I think this will help,' he said to her.

But they weren't safe for long. It was soon spotted that two of the party were not joining in and Fi and Rachel arrived to drag them onto the makeshift dance floor next to all the other flesh.

'No!' they both protested as they grabbed their wrists.

'No!' said Katy, remembering that Ben had told her that under no circumstances must she let Ollie dance, given that he was the worst dancer in the world.

But it was too late.

They were in amongst the thrusters and twerkers looking at each other in terror. They had no choice, they had to move. They had to dance. They were committed.

Despite the cocktail and two shots, the alcohol was fighting a losing battle against the terror of the situation and Katy found it impossible to get with the rhythm. She swayed awkwardly, hearing her own heartbeat thumping in her ears. Then she heard uproarious laughter coming from her left and watched as Rachel and Fi pointed at Ollie and his very awkward approach to musical movement.

He stopped suddenly when he spotted that he was being laughed at.

'I'm being the mother of the bride,' he announced.

They stopped for a moment then laughed again.

'You are a genius,' they told him, clapping him on the back. He grimaced and carried on.

I wish they'd play some Abba, thought Katy after about fifteen minutes of monotonous dancing to nameless tunes that if she were twenty years younger she might have heard of but to her mature ears just sounded like 'noise'. She was reminded of her dad complaining about *Top of the Pops* when she was a kid and telling her it was just *noise* and cupping his ears. How had she got as old as her dad?

She needed a break. It felt like she had been dancing for hours but she daren't leave Ollie to the rest of the hens, they might eat him alive. She looked at a bench longingly. Perhaps she would see if Ollie wanted a sit-down for a while. Take the weight off his feet.

She was about to sidle over to him when she spotted that Abby was missing again. This was absolutely the last time she was going to offer to play babysitter. She looked around and eventually spotted her dancing with a man. A man with perfectly groomed hair, shaped to an elaborate quiff, and a perfectly smooth honey-bronzed chest attached to buff biceps that pumped to the music. He could easily be described as the absolute polar opposite of Braindead. Katy gasped. What should she do now? Grab Abby by the scruff of the neck and demand that she sit quietly by Katy's side for the rest of the trip with her legs crossed? She was only dancing. That was okay, wasn't it? You could dance with a man when you were married. There wasn't a law against that, was there? But maybe there was when the man in question was thrusting his bits towards you in a predatory fashion. Maybe that was a step too far.

Fi, of all people, saved her in the end.

'Game time!' she declared, pumping her fist in the air. 'More drinks and game time.'

The rest of the girls cheered and trooped off the dance floor as one, taking Katy, Ollie and Abby with them towards the back of the boat to get more drinks and presumably play some hen party games that could be no worse than the torture of more dancing. And at least that would get Abby away from the lecherous men leering at her voluptuous cleavage.

She was wrong. Everything was about to get much worse.

It didn't take long for drinks to miraculously appear, resulting in them all chugging near-neat vodka quickly to quench the thirst they had achieved through dancing.

'So how come you're here on your own then, Ollie?' asked Rachel. 'You got no friends?'

'No, I, er… I, er… I, er… was supposed to be on my honeymoon but my fiancée changed her mind.'

'What? You didn't get married?' gasped Fi.

'No,' said Ollie, looking at his feet.

'So this should have been your honeymoon and instead you are on my hen do?' gasped Cassie.

'It would appear so, yes,' he replied.

'Blimey,' said Fi. 'That's got to be like some seriously bad karma, hasn't it? Having a jilted fiancé on your hen do, that would freak me out.'

'I don't think it's catching,' said Ollie.

Katy looked at Cassie, who had gone very pale.

'I'm so sorry,' said Cassie. 'Must have been absolutely devastating.'

'It was!' said Ollie bluntly.

Nooo, thought Katy. Don't tell her that.

'But you've survived, haven't you, Ollie?' she said. 'You realise it was the right thing. If she didn't love you then it was a good thing you didn't get married.'

Ollie stared back at her.

Too blunt perhaps, thought Katy.

'Yes,' he said eventually. 'Yes, it probably was.'

'You wouldn't want to be married to someone who didn't love you, would you?' continued Katy. Was she going too far now?

Ollie stared at her again and she noticed Cassie was hanging onto his every word.

'No,' he said firmly, a hint of determination in his voice. 'No, I wouldn't.'

'It's got to be time for Dickhead hoopla now, hasn't it?' declared Fi. 'Especially as we have Ollie as our special guest. He can be the Dickhead and we can all play hoopla with him.'

Katy felt sick and she was sure it wasn't the alcohol that she had consumed.

'Come on, get it out, Ruth,' urged Rachel. 'We all said we were going to play Dickhead hoopla on the boat. Get it out, now.'

'I'm not sure that's fair on Ollie actually,' said Cassie.

'Come on,' said Fi. 'If we have a man in our midst, he has to be the Dickhead surely? It's a gift, don't you think, girls?'

They all nodded and soon a chant of 'Dickhead, Dickhead, Dickhead, Dickhead' started to gather momentum as Ruth delved in her bag of tricks and pulled out whatever monstrosity was about to befall poor old Ollie.

Katy dared not look at him.

A plastic penis emerged attached to a piece of elastic and for one horrifying moment, Katy thought Ollie was going to be further humiliated by having to wear a strap-on. Then Ruth pulled out some brightly coloured rings about the diameter of an orange. What on earth were they going to do with them? Katy shivered.

'It's just hoopla,' Ruth said to Ollie. 'That's all. This goes on your head and we all throw rings at you to see if you can catch them on the... you know the...'

'Penis!' shrieked Fi, howling with laughter.

'If you don't want to do it, that's fine,' Cassie said. 'He doesn't have to do it, does he, Katy?' she said to her desperately as the chanting started again.

'Dickhead, Dickhead, Dickhead...' it began.

Ollie looked round him bewildered, then thrust the plastic penis on his head and looked back up, sweat pouring off his head.

Katy thought she might cry. How had she got Ollie into such a humiliating situation? She was supposed to be looking after him. Or was she? No, that was Abby. She was supposed to be improving Ollie's confidence with women! And now here he was, standing in front of her with a plastic penis on his head, with a load of girls chanting 'Dickhead' at him. Never had a night gone so terribly wrong.

Katy watched from between her fingers as the girls proceeded to throw plastic rings at Ollie's head.

It will be over soon, she thought, and then she would whisk him away and they would both go and hide in a corner somewhere until they got back to shore. She would console him and promise that life could not get any worse than this.

But then, it did.

Suddenly they were joined by the group of men who had been bumping and grinding with the girls on the upper deck. They took one look at the high jinks and soon the muscle men were throwing plastic rings at Ollie too. This was utterly terrible. Katy had to get him out of there. This could scar him for life, quite literally. Imagine getting an injury whilst playing Dickhead hoopla and having to say that was why. Utterly devastating.

Then she watched in horror as the oily guy who had clearly taken a liking to Abby snaked his arm around her waist and took aim at Ollie. She wasn't sure if Abby was welcoming this attention or she was just going with the flow, either way, if Braindead saw her, Katy was sure he wouldn't be happy.

In the end, it was Cassie who came to the rescue. She'd tried to end the game several times by bravely standing in front of Ollie and waving her arms around but everyone had ignored her and just thrown the rings over her head. She'd even told Ruth that she thought as the bride-to-be that she should take a turn as Dickhead but Ruth just laughed at her and said that a man being the Dickhead was much more entertaining. Eventually Cassie shouted, 'Let's do more shots!' at which point the crowd cheered and as one turned to the bar. Cassie nodded at Katy to take care of Ollie as she hustled them all away. The last thing she saw of Abby was her being hoisted on the man's shoulder in a fireman's lift and disappearing up the stairs. She was pounding his back with her fists and Katy wasn't sure if that was in protest or just *play* protest. Should she follow Abby and get her off that man's back or stay with Ollie? One look at Ollie and she knew she had to stay with him.

Trembling, Katy scrolled through her phone for Ben's number. She looked nervously over at Ollie, who was now breathing into a sick bag to try and calm down. He was pale and still wearing his Dickhead hoopla headwear, albeit cocked to one side at a jaunty angle.

She held the phone to her ear and prayed Ben had his phone with him.

'Hello,' he said in a surprised manner. 'Having fun? We're not. Jack, do not put French fries up your nose, especially not ones with ketchup on,' he shouted. 'Dinner has been a disaster. Millie didn't like the cheese they used in the carbonara so she ended up eating my steak, my entire steak, whilst I ate snotty spaghetti. How is your evening going?'

'Come and get us,' she whimpered.

'What did you say?'

'I said, come and get us.'

'Why? Aren't you pissed as a fart and doing the Macarena?'

'No,' gulped Katy. She didn't know where to start. 'It's like we have been violated,' she whimpered.

'Violated!' said Ben. 'What do you mean? No-one's touched you, have they? Because if they have, they will have me to deal with.'

'No, no, it's not me, it's just that... well, I don't know how it happened but they attached a penis to Ollie's head and threw things at him and now he's hyperventilating and Abby has just been carried away, and I mean literally carried away by some drunk knucklehead, and I didn't know who to stay with so I'm with Ollie because he may never breathe properly again but I really need to go and see if Abby is okay but I can't leave Ollie so please come and rescue us. We have to get off this boat.'

There was a silence at the end of the phone. Then she heard Ben speak to Braindead.

'Katy's upset,' he said. 'She wants us to go and fetch them. Ollie has a dick on his head and Abby... well, Abby has been carried away by some bloke.'

She didn't hear Braindead's response.

'Where are you?' Ben asked.

'In the middle of the sea,' she whimpered again.

'We're on our way,' he said after a slight pause and then the line went dead.

Chapter Twenty-One

They were at the harbour before they could both draw breath. It had been a hazardous journey, what with two toddlers in pushchairs and Millie trying to keep up. Then Braindead had suddenly shouted 'Nappy bag' at the front door of the hotel and had to dash back. Obviously an essential item when you were staging a rescue attempt.

They paused, trying to get their breath back.

'Can I have an ice cream?' asked Millie.

'No!' they both said in unison.

'Ice cream,' whined Logan.

'No!' said Braindead.

'Perlease,' he whined again. Braindead crouched down in front of him.

'Buddy, we are on a very important mission to save Mummy, do you hear? This is no time for ice cream,' said Braindead, standing up and looking out to sea. 'Do you think that's their boat?' he said, pointing.

About half a mile out to sea a boat was bobbing around with twinkly lights sparkling in the twilight. It looked as though it was packed with party revellers, dancing on the deck and jumping off the sides.

'Must be,' said Ben.

'We could swim there?' said Braindead.

'I don't think so,' said Ben.

'Pedalo!' shouted Braindead, looking down the beach. 'We could grab one of those and get to them that way.'

Ben stared at him.

'Do you not recall our disaster with the pedalo yesterday?' he said. 'We got precisely nowhere thanks to your steering. We went round in circles for forty minutes. I was actually seasick on a pedalo.'

'It was broken,' said Braindead. 'Must have been. Anyway, you got any better ideas?'

Ben looked round him. He spotted the small line of boats with outboard motors lined up along the harbour and a couple of men sitting on deckchairs next to them.

'Let's try them,' he said and headed down the length of the pier with Millie and Jack in tow.

'Do you speak English?' he asked.

The man shook his head.

Where was Gabriel when you needed him?

'We need to go there,' he urged, pointing at the boat on the sea.

The man looked out to sea, squinting, then shook his head.

'You take us there,' Ben said, pointing to the party boat and then to the boat next to them.

The man shrugged and returned to his card game.

Ben turned to face Braindead, at a loss, but he was on his phone.

'Gabriel, mate,' he said into his phone. 'Listen, we are in a bit of a pickle. Abby and Ollie are in trouble on the party boat and we need to rescue them. So we are at the harbour trying to hire a boat but the man doesn't understand our English. Can you tell him that we need him to take us to the boat out on the water?'

Braindead nodded his head, listening to Gabriel.

'I don't think they are in physical danger,' he said. 'It's just that Katy rang and said we needed to rescue them so we are down here with the kids, on our way.'

He nodded again and then passed the phone to the old man.

The old man took it reluctantly and listened, nodding his head. Then came a great avalanche of Spanish and then silence again. Ben held his breath. If anyone could convince an old Spanish man to take random men with kids to a party boat then Gabriel could. Couldn't he?

Eventually the man nodded again and returned the phone to Braindead.

'We go,' he said, nodding at the boat. 'Your friend will be here to pay me when we return or I keep one of the children,' he added. Then smiled.

'Right, kids,' said Ben, clapping his hands. 'This is an exciting adventure, right, isn't it? We are just going to get on this little boat and pick up your mummies and Ollie. Is that okay? Exciting, hey?'

'Ice cream when we get back,' said Millie, crossing her arms, 'or else I'm not getting in.'

'Yes,' said Ben with a deep sigh. 'Whatever you want, just get in the boat.'

The old man was handing out lifejackets, which of course took an age to put on the children as they wriggled and protested with their little bodies. Finally they were all in the boat and able to set off. The old man took up his oars and started to row.

'No, no,' said Braindead agitatedly. 'Motor! We need speed.'

'More money,' said the man, whose English seemed to be returning to him at a remarkable speed.

'Yes,' said Braindead. 'More money. Now for goodness' sake, get a move on.'

Chapter Twenty-Two

On our way x

Katy looked down at the text. She let out a sigh of relief. She peered out to sea and then irrationally peered up into the sky. Did she really think they were going to fly in by helicopter? She really had lost it.

Katy couldn't see anything coming across the water though. What exactly did Ben mean when he said they were on their way? Had they only just left the hotel? She could feel her heart starting to beat faster again. What if they took ages to arrive? She wasn't sure how long she could last in this situation.

Ollie had not emerged from the sick bag. In fact, when Katy tried to take it away from him, he clung to it, shaking his head vigorously as though it were some sort of security blanket. As though breathing into a sick bag somehow would prevent any further woe befalling him.

'Is it okay if I go upstairs and check on Abby?' she asked him. But he clutched her hand so tight that it hurt and his breathing increased so alarmingly that she daren't go anywhere.

She looked towards the shore again and thought she could see something heading towards them. A small vessel crowded with people in life jackets. It was like a scene from *Titanic*. She couldn't quite make out whether she recognised anyone in it but assumed it wasn't Ben, because why would he have brought so many people with him? She was just about to call him to ask exactly where he was when she thought she heard something. Something that she could recognise anywhere. Something that made her look sharply back to shore again.

Was that Jack crying?

She squinted her eyes, searching for other boats, but there weren't any apart from the overstuffed little dinghy.

Wait a minute. That looked like Millie's sunhat. The pink one. On the overstuffed boat. Oh God, it was all of them. All of them stuffed into a tiny boat heading out to their rescue. Ben, Millie, Jack, Braindead and Logan, she could see them all now. Logan and Jack were clasped in their dads' arms and Millie was at the front next to some old Spanish guy driving the boat. Why on earth had they brought the kids? Had they any idea what den of iniquity they were bringing them to?

'Here,' she began to shout, jumping up and down. 'Over here. I'm here. They're coming,' she said, looking down at Ollie. 'They've come to take us away.'

Ollie jumped up and looked out to sea. He took the bag away from his mouth.

'They brought the kids!' he exclaimed.

Chapter Twenty-Three

'Look, there's someone waving,' said Braindead, pointing at the boat. 'See at the back.'

'It's Katy!' said Ben. He raised both arms in the air, waving them vigorously. 'Katy!' he bellowed. 'Katy, we're coming.'

'Mummy!' shouted Millie, having now spotted her. 'Mummy! We're going to get ice cream.'

Ben leant forward and tapped the man on the shoulder and pointed to where Katy was. 'Over there, look,' he said.

The man nodded grimly, eyeing up the multitude of drunken swimmers that were now in his path. There was a continual drip feed of bodies jumping off the top deck into the water accompanied by shrieks and shouts. For the most part, they doggy-paddled around whilst occasionally trying to drag each other down before heading for the steps at the rear of the boat and hauling themselves back up for more drinking, dancing and diving.

'They're all semi-naked,' said Braindead in awe as they approached. 'Look, all of them.'

'You sound so old and married, mate,' said Ben.

'That looks fun,' said Millie. 'Can we do it?'

'No!' said Ben and Braindead in unison.

Then suddenly the old man cut the engine about fifty yards from the boat.

'What!' said Braindead. 'What are you doing?'

'Too dangerous,' said the man, shaking his head. 'Too many swimmers.'

'But we have to get to the boat. You said you'd take us to the boat.'

The man shrugged and sat down resolutely as the boat came to a standstill and everyone went quiet.

'Have we broken down?' said Millie. 'Are we going to drown, Daddy?'

'Of course not,' said Ben. 'We've just had to stop because of all these drunk people swimming. I mean, what are they thinking? What a ridiculous thing to do.'

'Now who's sounding old?' said Braindead.

'Mummy's still waving,' said Millie.

'What do we do now?' asked Braindead.

Chapter Twenty-Four

'They've stopped,' said Ollie. 'Why have they stopped?'

'I don't know,' replied Katy.

They stared out at the boat, trying to determine what was going on. Braindead appeared to be having an argument with the man in the front seat. He'd stood up and was waving his arms around but the man appeared to be ignoring him.

'Are you okay?' said a voice from behind them.

They both swivelled round to see Cassie standing there, looking distraught.

'It's all my fault,' she gasped. 'I can't believe they did that to you. And you just got jilted by your fiancée and everything. I'm so sorry.'

'It's not your fault,' said Ollie.

'But it is,' she continued. 'If I hadn't agreed to get married then this stupid hen do would never have happened and you would never have been stood on the deck of a boat whilst people shouted "Dickhead" at you.'

'This didn't happen because you agreed to get married,' said Katy, reaching forward to touch her arm.

'It did,' she replied. 'Me getting married is ruining everything.'

It was then that Katy heard a distant chant. She looked at Ollie nervously, her heart sinking to her stomach. 'Are they getting any closer?' she asked him.

Ollie turned to look over the side of the boat. 'They're still where they were,' he told her.

The chanting was beginning to get louder. Katy started talking gibberish to try and block out the noise. 'Maybe they're just discussing the weather and perhaps the man has received a bad forecast and is refusing to sail any further. Perhaps they've been listening to the shipping forecast and it said high winds due or whatever they say on the shipping forecast and they're deciding the next plan of action for our rescue and...'

She trailed off, as it was clear that Ollie wasn't listening to a word she was saying. His ears had pricked up and he was staring nervously at the steps leading up the top deck. The chant seemed to be getting much closer now as Ollie's face grew paler.

'Oh no,' muttered Cassie, looking scared.

'Dickhead, Dickhead, Dickhead,' came the cry, sounding as though it was approaching the top of the stairs.

The three of them watched as Fi's face appeared in the hole between the decks. She grinned. 'There's my little Dickhead,' she shouted across at Ollie before disappearing again. 'He's here,' they heard her shout across the top deck. 'Come on, girls.'

Katy looked at Ollie, whose face had completely drained of colour. They stared at each other for a moment. Fi was now making her way down the steps. Katy could see the panic rising in Ollie's face. He glanced back at Fi.

'Come to me, Dickhead,' she said, an evil glint in her eye.

'No way!' he shouted. He turned, hauled himself up onto the railing and jumped overboard.

'Oh fuck!' said Katy.

'No!' shrieked Cassie.

They both dashed to the railing and leaned over, looking down into the water. Katy couldn't see him. Where had he gone? Then she was aware of Cassie climbing up onto the rail beside her.

'No!' Katy shouted, trying to grab hold of Cassie's arm but it was too late. Cassie jumped and the next moment there was an almighty splash.

Now what? Katy had no choice. She had to go after them. Besides, Fi was going to get here any second and anything was better than facing her. She climbed onto the railing and launched herself off the side of the boat with an almighty scream.

Chapter Twenty-Five

'Man overboard,' cried Braindead, standing up. 'Man overboard! Ollie just jumped. He jumped off the boat, did you see him?'

Ben had been momentarily distracted by an argument that had erupted between Millie and Jack over Millie's hat. Jack had swiped it and Millie was none too happy about it. But indeed, Ben could see that Ollie had vanished from the railing from which he had previously been waving, and there stood Katy and another lady peering down into the water.

'What! He just jumped?' said Ben. 'Just like that?'

'Yeah,' replied Braindead. 'Just climbed on the side and jumped.'

'Oh my God, Katy!' said Ben, watching in a daze as a lady he didn't recognise followed by his wife clambered onto the top of the railing. 'What is she doing? Crikey, I can't watch.'

'Wow!' said Millie. 'Is that Mummy?'

They all stared as Katy flew through the air, her arms flailing. She let out an ear-piercing scream as she hit the water. There was a big splash and then silence.

'Right, that's it,' said Braindead. 'I'm going in. I'll go and see if they're all right, then I'm going to fetch my wife.'

'I'll come too,' said Ben.

'No! Someone needs to stay with the kids,' said Braindead, unbuttoning his shirt to reveal his quite pale and slightly flabby body. 'Abby led everyone into this so it's my job to sort it out.' He kicked off his sandals and stepped to the edge of the boat before raising his hands above his head in preparation for a dive.

'Wish me luck,' he said.

'Good luck, buddy,' said Ben. 'Bring them back safe.'

'I will,' he said, then belly-flopped into the sea.

Ben looked back towards the party boat. He could see Katy's and Ollie's heads bobbing around in the water. They'd emerged from their dive. That was good. There were also three or four women gathered at the rail where they had stood previously, shouting down at them. He couldn't quite hear what they were saying. He thought they might be shouting 'Dickhead' which felt harsh but it really did sound like that. He reached forward and covered Millie's ears.

*

'What the hell is going on?' asked Braindead, swimming up to Katy and Ollie. 'Are you okay?'

'We are now,' said Katy.

'Why are they shouting "Dickhead" at you?' said Braindead, joining them in doggy-paddle.

They all looked up to the boat, where Fi and Rachel were chanting down, pointing at Ollie.

'It's all my fault,' said Cassie, bobbing up behind them.

'No, it's not,' said Katy. 'It's Cassie's hen party,' she explained to Braindead. 'This is Abby's husband,' she told Cassie.

'Pleased to meet you,' said Braindead, 'I'd shake your hand but…'

'I'm so sorry to have put you to this trouble,' interrupted Cassie.

'Where's Abby?' asked Braindead.

'She's still on there,' said Katy. 'She... she got carried away by this bloke and we haven't seen her since.'

Braindead nodded grimly.

'Can you swim to the boat?' he said to the three of them. 'He wouldn't get any closer because of all the swimmers. Do you think you can make it?'

'Sure,' said Ollie.

'I think so,' said Katy.

'Only if there's room for me,' said Cassie. 'If not, then I guess I'll just hang out here for a bit. I always did great doggy-paddle.'

'Don't be so ridiculous,' said Katy. 'You're coming with us.'

'Right,' said Braindead. 'I'll go and get Abby.'

*

Braindead could hear his heart pounding as he swam towards the rear of the boat, where there was a ladder that the swimmers were using to get back on board. There were bikini-clad women squealing all around him and he could now hear the thumping music. Fortunately the girls seemed to have ceased their chant of 'Dickhead'.

He closed his eyes for a moment as he lined up behind a bikini bottom climbing up the ladder – he really didn't need to see that. Eventually he got onto the steps and hauled himself up, looking around at the heaving mass of bodies swaying to music and downing drinks. He wasn't sure how he was going to find his wife amongst all this lot.

He started methodically. Walking up and down the deck in parallel lines almost as if he were a policeman seeking evidence. He was worried that he would get accused of staring at the semi-naked bodies and so tried really hard to keep his eyes at head level despite the cleavages regularly being thrust in his face.

He couldn't see Abby anywhere and then he caught sight of the women who had been chanting from the rails. They must be part of the hen party, he thought, and might know where Abby was. He strode over.

'Where's Abby?' he asked gruffly.

'Oooh,' said Fi, staring at him. 'You are ever so demanding, aren't you?'

'Where is she?' he repeated.

'Well, you'll have to get in the queue because the last I saw of her she was attracting a lot of attention, if you know what I mean.'

'Tell me where she is,' he said again, taking a step forward and resisting the temptation to shake her.

'Why should I?' said Fi defiantly, tottering slightly on her heels.

'Because I'm her husband,' stated Braindead.

'Ooooooo,' drawled Fi. 'Of course you are. I remember you now. Well, the last time I saw her, she was upstairs at the back with a rugby team from Middlesbrough.'

Braindead turned and flew up the stairs two at a time.

He got to the top and looked around wildly. He couldn't see her. Where was she?

'Abby!' he bellowed, cupping his hands around his mouth. 'Abby!'

He listened but there was no reply.

'Abby,' he shouted again over the booming music. 'Abby!'

'Braindead!' he heard from his left. He swivelled round to see his wife pinned into a corner by a leery beefcake. He had his arm leaning over her head, making it difficult for her to move away.

'Braindead!' she shouted again.

He ran towards her and grabbed her hand, pulling her towards him.

'Oi, mate,' said the bloke. 'Who do you think you are?'

'Her husband,' said Braindead.

'I told you I was married,' said Abby. 'I did,' she said to Braindead. 'It isn't how it looks, we were just talking and then… and then he started saying things and… and I said I was married but he wouldn't believe me and he thought I was coming on to him but I wasn't and… and…'

Before she could continue Braindead lashed out and thumped the man square in the face. He stumbled back, falling to the floor, clasping his jaw.

Braindead turned to Abby. 'If you want to stay, you can stay,' he said. 'If this is what you want?'

She shook her head. 'Of course it isn't.' She started to cry. Braindead watched as she sank her head into her hands.

'Then what do you want?' he asked, feeling exasperated. 'You don't want to spend any time with me or Logan. All you seem to want is to pretend that we don't even exist. To be out and acting like you're single again.'

Abby's shoulders rose and fell as she continued to cry then she raised her head.

'I do want to be with you, honestly I do, and Logan, it's just…' she petered off, clearly struggling with what to say.

'Just what?' he demanded. 'You have to tell me. Whatever this is, it's stopping you being happy. It's stopping me being happy.'

'I miss being me and you,' she said. 'Me and you… we were fun… me and you have… gone.'

Braindead was at a loss. None of it made any sense. He hadn't gone anywhere. What did she mean?

The man was now struggling to his feet, clutching his jaw and looking menacingly at Braindead. He needed answers but he suspected that now wasn't the time.

Braindead grabbed Abby's hand and yanked her away. 'Let's go,' he said. They dashed towards the stairs and galloped down them, landing on the lower deck with a thump.

'Are you okay to swim?' Braindead said to Abby.

'Yes,' she gasped, looking nervously behind her.

'Right,' he said. 'Let's get out of here.'

He dragged them both towards the railing and helped Abby to climb up and he swiftly followed. On top, he took her hand and looked at her.

'Ready?' he asked.

'Ready,' she replied.

Then they jumped, screaming as they did so.

Chapter Twenty-Six

'They just jumped in,' said Katy, pointing at the boat.

Katy, Ollie and Cassie had made it to the rescue boat and been hauled out the water by Ben whilst the old man held onto Logan and Jack and kept an eye on Millie.

'What the hell happened?' asked Ben as they sat down panting. Ollie still had the 'Dickhead' penis attached to his head, but it was now sticking out sideways.

'What is that?' asked Millie, pointing.

'Willy!' shouted Logan. 'Willy!'

Ollie grasped at his head then fumbled with the plastic clip under his chin before tearing it off.

'What is it?' asked Millie again.

'An instrument of torture,' muttered Ollie, throwing it out to sea with all his might.

'Willy, bye,' said Logan, waving.

'It wasn't a willy,' said Millie sternly. 'It doesn't look anything like Daddy's and you don't get willy hats anyway, do you, Daddy?'

'No, Millie,' said Ben. 'That's right. Just forget you saw it, okay? It's nothing to worry about.'

'But why was it on Ollie's head?' asked Millie. 'It looked silly.'

'Why was it on your head?' asked Ben.

'They made me do it,' said Ollie.

'Who did?'

'Them,' he said, pointing to the boat. 'Those girls on there. They made me wear it and then they threw stuff at me.'

'What sort of stuff?'

'Rings and then other stuff. Anything they could get their hands on and then some boys joined in and then they threw things at me.'

'You were bullied!' said Millie with a gasp. 'That's not allowed. You need to tell your teacher. People can't throw things at you. That's bullying.'

'You're right, Millie,' said Ollie.

'We'll sort it,' said Katy, putting her arm round her daughter. 'Don't worry, they won't get away with it and you're right. If you get bullied, you must always tell a teacher. Do you understand?'

Millie gave her a weird look.

'Of course,' she replied. 'I just told you that.'

'I'm so sorry,' said Cassie, who had been sitting with her head in her hands. 'It's all my fault.'

'It wasn't your fault,' said Ollie sternly.

'But it was my hen party. I should never have let it get that far,' she protested.

'You were brave,' continued Ollie. 'You saved me from Dickhead hoopla.'

'Phrases you thought you'd never say on your honeymoon,' muttered Ben.

Ollie looked at Ben and swallowed. 'Along with "I'm glad I'm alone on honeymoon because now I realise my fiancée didn't love me."'

'That's the spirit!' cried Ben, slapping him on the back. 'I'm going to get you a T-shirt with that printed on it from that shop in the market.'

'Thank you for coming to get us,' Ollie said. 'Seriously. Thank you.'

'Yes,' said Cassie. 'I know you don't know me but thank you for rescuing me from my own hen party.'

'You're welcome,' replied Ben.

'I think they both needed saving,' said Katy to Ben as she reached out and touched his hand whilst giving Millie and Jack an extra-special squeeze.

Chapter Twenty-Seven

'Here you go, Abby,' shouted Ben. 'Take my hand.'

Abby swam towards the boat and grasped Ben's hand. He hauled her in swiftly, followed by Braindead. They both collapsed on the bottom of the boat, gasping.

'Mummy,' said Logan, scrambling over Ben to join her.

Abby looked up, tears visibly flooding her eyes.

'Logan,' she said, throwing her arms open and hugging him to her chest, tears spilling down her cheeks and onto his head.

*

No-one said anything on the short trip back to the shore. Not even Millie, Logan or Jack. They left the thumping music of the party boat behind them and were grateful for the relative peace of the quiet shoreline.

As they approached the harbour they could see Daniel, Gabriel and Silvie waiting for them, looking somewhat apprehensive.

'Your friends?' asked the old man in the boat.

'Yes,' said Ben. 'Our friends.'

'He speak Spanish?' asked the man.

'He does,' said Ben.

They moored up to the harbour and one by one climbed out of the boat onto the wooden pier.

'Literally shipwrecked,' said Daniel, his eyes wide open, eyeing them all up.

Gabriel asked the old man a question in Spanish and he replied with much waving of hands and incredulity. He gestured to them all, clearly giving his own version of events.

'What is he saying?' asked Daniel when the old man finally seemed to have finished his story.

'He said these English people are mad, crazy people. He has no idea what just happened but a man jumped off a big boat with a penis attached to his head and in seventy years, he has never had such a bizarre experience. Oh, and we owe him fifty euros,' he finished.

Gabriel reached for his wallet but Braindead got in first, thrusting notes into the man's hand.

'Thank you,' he said, shaking his hands. 'Thank you so much.'

The man came out with another stream of Spanish.

They all looked at Gabriel expectantly, waiting for him to translate.

'He says he has had an enjoyable adventure.'

They all nodded silently.

'I think it's time for bed,' said Katy, looking around at all the exhausted faces.

'Good idea,' muttered Ben.

'Braindead, why don't you take the honeymoon suite? You and Abby. We'll look after Logan tonight. He'll be fine with us,' said Katy.

Braindead stared at her for a moment before muttering a thank you. He hoisted Logan into his arms and then took his wife's hand as they headed back towards the hotel.

*

Changing rooms again was not as simple as it could have been. Katy and Ben walked back into the honeymoon suite where they had lain on the bed earlier and talked about their night so excitedly. She knew it was entirely the right thing to do to let Braindead and Abby have the honeymoon suite, they needed time alone, but nonetheless she had been looking forward to sleeping in the kingsize bed even if that was the only thing that would be happening in it. She stuffed her still-soaking-wet dress into a carrier bag and slung it onto the top of the case before putting on her pyjamas. What a ridiculous night it had been.

To top everything off, there had been an altercation in the hallway while the kids' cots were transported late at night. As Ben and Braindead tried to manoeuvre a cot into the lift, a porter had suddenly appeared and started shouting at them in Spanish, waving his arms around. Of course, the cot got jammed and the only option was to go and find Gabriel to translate to the poor porter that they were not trying to steal the cot, they were merely trying to save their friends' marriage. The porter looked somewhat dubious at this explanation and remained stuck to Ben's side until finally two cots and three children were safely installed in their bedroom.

'Want Daddy,' said Logan to Katy as she shut the door and wondered how on earth they were going to settle three children and get some sleep. It was ten o'clock.

'He's with Mummy, sweetheart,' she said to him. 'You're having a sleepover with us just for tonight and do you know what we are going to do because it's a special sleepover?'

'No!' said Logan, his eyes wide.

'Just because you are here we are all going to get into bed and watch cartoons as a special treat until you go to sleep.'

'*Tractor Ted*?' asked Logan.

'Yes,' said Katy. 'Of course, but only if you get your pyjamas on super quick and get into bed.'

'That bed?' he said, pointing to their bed.

Katy looked at him and thought she might cry.

'I wouldn't if I were you,' said Ben to Logan. 'Katy is the worst snorer and she farts,' he told him.

'Mummy not fart,' said Logan with a frown.

'This one does,' he said, pointing his finger at Katy. 'Like a trooper. You are better off in your own bed, mate. Believe me. Now go and brush your teeth quick.'

'I do not fart in bed!' said Katy crossly.

'Did you want Logan wriggling next to you all night?'

'No.'

'Well then.'

She threw a pillow at Ben.

'And so ends our romantic night,' she told him.

*

Braindead finally shut the door of the honeymoon suite when all the sleeping arrangements had been settled. He paused with his hand on the door handle. He was so tired.

He turned round and trudged into the main room with the enormous kingsize bed and the beautiful view of the bay. It was even nicer than the honeymoon suite they'd had on their own honeymoon, he thought. Poor Ollie. It must have been something close to torture sleeping in here.

Abby was sitting on the edge of the bed, her head in her hands. She hadn't really said anything since they got out of the water. She'd sat shivering next to him on the boat, clutching Logan on her knee as though she was in her own world. When they got back to the hotel she had packed her bag in silence and made her own way to the honeymoon suite before kissing Logan goodbye. Then she had fled to the bathroom and locked herself in whilst Braindead took Logan down to Ben and Katy's room.

Braindead sat down slowly beside her. A million questions flew through his head but he didn't know where to start. He had no idea what frame of mind she was in. The truth was he'd had no idea for some time.

'I'm sorry,' Abby muttered through her fingers. 'I'm so sorry.'

'What for?' asked Braindead.

She took her head out of her hands, taking a deep breath.

'For being an utter cow.'

Braindead said nothing. She *had* been a cow. It was a fact.

They both stared ahead.

'Why have you been a cow?' he ventured. He couldn't go, 'There, there, it's okay,' because it wasn't: it was not okay.

She turned to look at him and he watched as her face crumpled. Ugly crumpled. He had never seen her like that before. She looked like someone was forcing an invisible hand over her face and squashing it up.

She heaved and then began to sob.

He couldn't watch and do nothing. He reached forward, pulled her to his chest and held her. Held her until the sobs grew less. Held her while he wondered whether they were going to survive this storm.

It was some time before Abby recovered enough to raise her head to reveal a river of streaked mascara and snot running down her still-crumpled face.

Braindead got up and went into the bathroom to fetch some tissues. He couldn't find any so he brought out a wet flannel, which he'd added too much water to. It dripped all the way through the bathroom and bedroom and then onto Abby.

'Thank you,' she muttered, taking it off him and wiping her face. Water dripped profusely onto her knees.

She looked at it when she'd finished, wondering where to put it. Her face was now soaking wet and she needed a towel.

'Give me a minute,' she said, getting up and going back into the bathroom.

When she came back, Braindead was still standing up. Too restless to sit down, he was practically pacing the room.

Abby dropped down on the bed and took a deep breath.

'I don't know what's been wrong with me,' she said. 'I… I just I don't know what I'm doing. I'm a terrible mother, I know I am and I'm so sorry. I just can't do it and I know I should know what to do but every time I look at Logan I just panic and… and… I freeze and I'm so scared that I'll do it wrong and that would be a disaster so it's just easier to let you do it because you're so much better than me and… and I'm scared, Braindead, all the time. I feel scared and I'm never scared but I have this feeling in my tummy that won't go away and I think it's fear but I don't really know but it makes me feel sick and then… and then…' she paused, looking down at the floor, kicking her toe against the carpet.

'And when I wake up in the morning the feeling is really bad and I don't want to get up.' She looked up at Braindead, tears flooding her eyes at this admission. 'I don't want to get up. I dread going to sleep because then morning will come and I'll wake up and I know I won't want to get up and I feel so sick and I don't know what to do about that. Because I feel so terrible but I don't know why really. I just feel so unhappy.'

She sank her head into her hands again.

Braindead looked down at her.

She looked up suddenly.

'Do you still want to be married to me?' she said, tears rolling down her cheeks.

'Yes!' said Braindead without hesitation or thought. 'Of course I do,' he added, taking a seat beside her again and putting his arm around her. 'Do you still want to be married to me?'

She turned to look at him but didn't speak. Braindead thought his heart might stop.

'Yes,' she eventually whispered. 'Of course I do.'

They both cried and rocked on the edge of the bed.

'But you looked happy talking to that man,' said Braindead eventually, fighting back the tears. 'You've looked happy this week going out with those girls.'

Abby started to shake her head.

'I kind of was. I was trying to be the me that I was before we got married,' she said. 'I thought that might help. I thought if I could pretend I was that me again then I might be happy again and I sort of was, and it was good to get drunk and forget everything for a while, and it even made me feel good to have men chat me up.' She looked down, ashamed. 'I kept thinking I'd found myself again, you know. That I knew who I was again. I know how to go out and have a good time on a night out. I just don't know how to be a good mum or a good wife and... and I feel like a total failure.'

'No,' said Braindead. 'You're not a failure. Don't ever think that. Marrying you was the happiest day of my life along with the day Logan arrived. You gave me all that. How can you be a failure?'

'But you don't need me any more,' she said. 'You don't want me even.'

'What do you mean? Of course I want you.'

She looked back up into his eyes. 'You don't look at me how you used to,' she said.

'I do.'

'You don't. You look at me like… like I am just a mum… not your wife, not the woman you married.'

Braindead stared back at her and swallowed.

'You don't want to spend any time with just me. All you care about is spending time with Logan. I'm jealous, Braindead. Of our son!'

Abby buried her head in her hands again and started to sob quietly.

Braindead rubbed her back, fighting back the tears himself.

'I'm sorry,' he murmured over and over. 'I'm sorry.'

When she finally seemed to calm down he gently grasped her shoulders and lifted her up so he could see her face. He wiped a tear from her left eye and then her right.

'You're a mess,' he said.

'I know,' she agreed.

'But you're *my* mess,' he said, putting a strand of hair behind her ear. 'My most beautiful, gorgeous, sexy mess that ever there was.'

'Really?' she asked. 'Do you really think that?'

'Of course I do,' he replied. 'I love you so much and all I want is for you to be happy.'

'I'm sorry I'm not happy,' she replied looking down.

He tipped her chin back up towards him with his hand so she had to look at him. 'We're going to work that out,' he told her. 'Together. I married *you* Abby. The love of my life. We'll work it out. It's what we promised to do the day we got married.'

She gazed into his eyes for a second longer before she smiled a watery smile and whispered, 'I love you.' Then the tears started to flow again.

He held her and she held him back until they slowly lay down together in the honeymoon suite.

Chapter Twenty-Eight

Ben had set his alarm for the following day. They'd found that getting up at 7 a.m. and getting into breakfast early was by far the best way to ensure that they managed to have a calm and peaceful meal. It had taken them nearly a week of trial and error to work this out.

None of the kids were awake so Ben and Katy crept into the bathroom to do their ablutions and then one by one gently woke the three children. They changed nappies, pulled on shorts and T-shirts, brushed teeth and were standing in front of the lift by 7.30 a.m. with three still bleary-eyed children.

'Do you think we're early enough?' asked Ben, nervously looking at his watch.

'Hope so,' yawned Katy. 'I need about twelve cups of coffee today.'

The lift door pinged open, revealing an elderly couple looking very bright and breezy for this time in the morning.

'Which number?' asked Millie, taking her station by the buttons.

'Zero,' said Katy, giving the elderly couple a warm smile.

'Will Uncle Braindead and Auntie Abby be at breakfast?' asked Millie.

'Maybe not just yet,' replied Katy.

'Maybe they stayed up late watching *Peppa Pig* too,' said Millie.

'Maybe,' said Katy.

'Can we do that again tonight? *Peppa Pig*, I mean,' asked Millie, 'or are we only allowed when Logan's mummy and daddy have had an argument and might get divorced?'

The woman in the lift looked up at Katy sharply.

'What's 'vorced?' asked Jack.

'It's when mummies and daddies don't like each other any more,' said Millie before Katy could step in.

'But there's no need to worry about that,' said Katy. 'That's not going to happen to Logan's mummy and daddy.'

There was quiet for a moment.

'If Logan sleeps with us tonight, can we watch *Peppa Pig* until midnight again?' asked Millie.

'Oh look, we've arrived,' declared Ben, dashing out of the lift like his bottom was on fire. 'Quick, kids,' he shouted over his shoulder. 'We need to get our seats.'

Katy tried to maintain her dignity and leave the lift in an orderly manner but she did jostle the elderly man in her desire to get in front of the couple in the queue for breakfast.

As she walked through the doors into the dining room with Logan still in her arms, she looked over to their favourite seats and sighed with relief to see Ben waving back at her triumphantly. She made her way over to the coveted area, which had a large table in the window next to a small child-height table ideal for the toddlers and for Millie. But best of all it was positioned next to a screen playing cartoons so that the adults could eat in peace whilst the kids were occupied. Utter bliss and so worth getting up at 7 a.m. in the morning for whilst on holiday. Just for a bit of peace at breakfast time.

'Well done,' she said to Ben, plopping down her bag and letting Logan down. 'Do you want to go and fetch their breakfast whilst I wait here? But could you just grab me a coffee first and then all will be well.'

'You betcha,' said Ben, diving off to the coffee machine then depositing a cup in front of her before going off in search of a plateful of carbs to keep the kids happy for at least half an hour.

We've nailed this, thought Katy. Just as we get near to the end of our holiday. Perhaps they should have booked for two weeks and then they might have had half a chance of enjoying the second week, having worked out how to do everything. Or maybe not.

'Oh, well done,' said Daniel, approaching with Silvie and Gabriel. 'We thought we might have missed it but I said to Gabriel I thought you'd be on it, given you have three kids with you. And you got a high chair. There you go, Silvie.'

'How did you sleep?' asked Gabriel, looking concerned.

'Funnily enough, like an angel,' replied Katy. 'I think all the excitement must have worn me out.'

'Any sign of Braindead and Abby yet?' asked Daniel.

'No,' said Katy, shaking her head. 'I think they will want to be down soon,' she added. 'Braindead doesn't like to be parted from Logan for too long, does he?'

'They will have had much to talk about hopefully,' said Gabriel. 'I hope they talked all night and are exhausted. That is what they need.'

'We shall see,' said Katy. 'We shall see.'

'Morning,' said Ben, arriving back at the table. 'I have Silvie's customary pancake here,' he said, setting a plate down in front of her. 'For Madame. Enjoy,' he said, smiling at her.

'By the way,' he then whispered to Katy. 'There's Nutella by the toast section, so I've hidden it under the jam for safe-keeping until you're ready for it.' She had been most upset that for the last two days it had run out before she got to the toast course of her breakfast. 'Why don't you go and get yours and I'll sort out this lot,' he said, nodding at the kids.

Half an hour later and they were having a civilised conversation about hanging baskets whilst the children played with their leftover food and spat milk at each other. Katy thought this might actually be the high point of their holiday.

Braindead and Abby appeared hand in hand at the door and looked around.

'Over here,' shouted Ben, standing up and waving.

'Holding hands,' muttered Daniel under his breath.

'I know,' said Katy, silently praying that was a good sign.

'You look knackered,' said Ben, looking them up and down. 'Good night in the bridal suite, was it?'

Katy groaned. What was her husband thinking? She doubted very much if Braindead had made full use of the bridal suite. Very much indeed. Indeed it was clearly destined that none of them were to make proper use of it.

'How are you feeling?' Katy asked Abby, who had so far been looking furtively at the ground.

'I'm okay,' she said quietly. 'I'm sorry,' she blurted out. 'For making you go out and everything. I'm so sorry.'

'Oh, Abby!' said Katy, standing up and putting her arms around her. 'It's okay.' They stood there for a long time whilst Katy looked over her shoulder at Braindead. He mouthed 'Thank you' at her.

'We'd like to take you all out for a meal tonight,' said Abby, pulling away. 'On us. All of us and the kids.'

'Yes!' exclaimed Gabriel. 'What a marvellous idea. And I know just the place. The man on the boat recommended somewhere. Somewhere with real Spanish food. Where the locals go. He said it has the best food in the region and the best wine, naturally.'

'Oh, that sounds perfect,' said Katy, laughing. 'Wow, how exciting. Proper Spanish food, not pizza and chips. Do they do paella, do you think?' she asked Gabriel. 'I've been dying for a decent paella ever since we got here.'

'They will cook whatever they think is best that day. But it will be absolutely delicious, I'm sure,' replied Gabriel.

'Has anyone seen Ollie?' said Abby. 'I need to find him and invite him. He should come with us. I feel so bad about what they did to him on the boat.'

'I think he would love a civilised meal with us,' said Katy. Then she suddenly had a thought as she recalled the night before. 'Can I invite one more person?' she said.

'Who?' asked Abby.

'I'll tell you later, but is that okay? I think they need a decent night out as well and… and I think they would enjoy our company.'

'Invite who you like,' said Braindead. 'Let's just enjoy ourselves, hey? I think it's well overdue.'

'One last thing,' said Ben. He glanced over at Braindead.

'What?'

'Any chance we can have the honeymoon suite tonight?' he asked, winking at Katy.

Chapter Twenty-Nine

'So I rang ahead,' said Gabriel as they all gathered in the reception of the hotel that evening. 'And it so happens that the owner knows my dad.'

'Oh my God,' said Katy. 'How random is that?'

'Well, in Spain we have many generations of restaurateurs and bar owners and so everyone knows everyone and there are lots of people who marry other people in the profession, you know. Apparently Francisco was at a wedding of his niece five years ago and Dad was there as a friend of the groom's father. They got drunk together.'

'Wow,' said Katy. 'Still crazy.'

'Anyway, Francisco has set up the best table for us all and very much looks forward to meeting everyone. I called my dad and he said we were going to be treated like kings.'

'Isn't my husband amazing?' said Daniel, full of smug pride.

'I actually think he rather is,' agreed Katy, thinking that Gabriel had saved the day on more than one occasion on this holiday.

'Did you send the address to your guest?' Gabriel asked Katy.

'I did,' she replied. 'I'm hoping she will come but I'm not entirely sure. She may feel she has other commitments.'

'Is she a Spanish pen pal or something?' asked Daniel. 'Why have you not mentioned her before?'

'No, nothing like that. Just someone who needs a bit of a break and who I thought might enjoy a relatively calm evening.'

'Taxis are here,' shouted Braindead from the doorway. He was clutching Abby's hand. She looked fragile but beautiful in a maxi dress with her hair pulled back and minimal make-up. A world away from the hen party glam of the night before. She smiled at Katy.

'You okay?' Katy asked her as they tried to hustle everyone out of the building.

'I think I'm going to be,' she said.

'I know you will,' replied Katy, squeezing her arm.

*

'I think I might cry,' said Daniel as they pulled up outside the remote shack on the headland about fifteen minutes later. There was nothing fancy about the restaurant, in fact it was quite tatty, but there were pots and pots of vibrant geraniums lining the veranda whilst vines intertwined along the roof terrace interspersed with sparkling fairy lights. Along the front was a long trestle table laid for twelve surrounded by mismatched chairs. The table was already crammed with plates and glasses and huge bowls of fresh bread. It looked absolutely delightful.

As they arrived, a man and woman came rushing up to them, babbling in Spanish, helping them out of their taxis and pumping their fists with vigorous handshakes. Gabriel found his way to the man and began talking to him and soon they were laughing and hugging as if they had known each other for years.

Gabriel introduced each of them individually to Francisco and his wife Sophia, saving his warmest introductions for the children. Both Francisco and Sophia oohed and aahed and miraculously produced little sweet lollipops, much to their delight, whilst dragging out some of the children who had been eating with their parents to come and take them off to the small makeshift sand box that was positioned in one corner of the veranda.

'Welcome,' said Francisco, opening his arms up. 'I am so delighted to have friends of Carlos here. You will come and sit and you will eat the best food you can eat in this town.'

'Can I tell him I love him yet?' asked Daniel, totally smitten.

'After I do,' said Katy, eagerly approaching the table and taking a seat next to her husband, from where she could see Jack and Millie playing.

'The beautiful lady here,' said Francisco, pulling out a chair for Abby. 'You will have the angel chair.'

Abby looked at him in awe and sat down and sighed. This was somewhere where you could forget all your woes for a time, Katy could tell. A very special place indeed.

'Now,' Francisco said, clapping his hands. 'You will help yourself to bread and wine and we will bring you food. Simple as that. No menu here, we bring you what is best. Put your trust in Sophia, she truly is the greatest chef there is here.'

'Oh my God,' said Katy. 'No tricky menus to decipher, no panicking about seats, no queuing for coffee. It just comes to you. I wish we had found this place earlier.'

They had just got settled when a taxi pulled up and they all squinted to see who would get out. They didn't recognise her at first as Cassie had ditched the short skirts and the high heels and was wearing a flowing skirt and T-shirt along with some oversized sunglasses. In fact it wasn't until she took her sunglasses off that Katy recognised her at all.

'Cassie!' she shouted, getting up. 'You came.'

'Cassie!' said Ollie, immediately standing up.

'She's the bride-to-be, right?' said Braindead, looking confused. 'The one who jumped off the boat with you?'

'That's right,' said Ollie. 'She saved me from the Dickhead hoopla.'

'So why isn't she with the hen party tonight?' said Ben.

'No idea,' said Ollie.

Katy dashed over to Cassie and wrapped her arms around her. She'd sent her a text earlier to ask if she fancied a hen-free night out and if there was any chance she could get a pass from her own hen party. The reply was emphatic.

Yes!!! I will be there. No-one can stop me, not even Ruth! Cassie xx

'So how did you get past Ruth?' asked Katy when they had finished hugging.

'I told her straight,' she said. 'Said that I hadn't enjoyed last night and it was awful what they did to your friend so I was having a night to myself and she could stuff it.'

'Check you out,' gasped Katy. 'So what are you missing then?'

'Magic Mike tribute troupe.'

'Wow, lucky escape,' she said. 'Come on over and sit down.

'So, I think most have you have met Cassie,' said Katy as they approached the table. 'Either out with the hen party or in the rescue boat last night.'

Everyone chorused their hellos and Cassie shyly waved back.

'I'm so sorry,' she said to Ollie, spotting him for the first time. 'I've been feeling so terrible about last night and I can't believe you ended up on your honeymoon, having not got married, with a bunch of crazy women shouting "Dickhead" at you, causing you to jump ship and have to be rescued by a man called Braindead.'

It was Braindead who laughed first. Laughed good and hard, which set everyone else off until even Ollie was clutching his sides.

'You have had the worst honeymoon in history,' declared Daniel, wiping the tears from his eyes. 'Like shockingly bad, like absolutely terrible. You've had a worse holiday than the rest of us.'

Ollie looked around at everyone smiling at him.

'I'm so very, very sorry,' Cassie said again, looking concerned.

'Do you know what?' said Ollie. 'It wasn't so bad. In fact… in fact it's been kind of fun. And if I'd have got married then I could be sat here next to a woman who was going to divorce me in a couple of years' time and that would have been a much more disastrous honeymoon.'

'Hear, hear,' said Ben, raising his glass.

'Hear, hear,' chimed in everyone.

'To not marrying the wrong person,' said Katy, raising her glass and trying not to look at Cassie.

'May your next honeymoon be with a woman who loves you,' added Gabriel. 'I think you will find someone sooner than you think.'

'Now why don't you sit down here?' said Katy to Cassie. 'Next to Ollie as he could be the only person around the table who won't be talking baby poo and he can tell you much more about how happy he is that his fiancée dumped him.'

'I'm delirious,' said Ollie to Cassie. 'Well, I'm surviving.'

'I never caught how you all know each other?' asked Cassie, taking a seat.

'Ollie was a stray we picked up on day one,' said Daniel. 'He was really lucky to bump into us.'

'Yeah,' agreed Ollie. 'They took my room, made me humiliate myself in a club and somehow got me involved in a game of Dickhead hoopla. It's been such a pleasure to meet you all, I must say.'

'That is all quite unfortunate,' said Daniel. 'But I would like to add that we brought you here.'

Ollie looked around and glanced at Cassie, who smiled at him.

'That's true,' he agreed. 'This might just make up for the mental torture from the rest of the week.'

'Calamari,' came the cry from Francisco as he approached the table with two plates laden with crispy quid. 'Caught this morning. The children have already tried some and approve.'

'Millie ate squid?' said Ben in shock, looking over to where she and Jack were both still happily playing with some other children, chasing each other round some flower pots. 'She normally won't stray past fish fingers at home!'

'Mummy!' came a cry followed by a wail.

All the parents in the group looked over immediately to see who the agonising wail had come from.

It was Logan, who was lying on the floor clutching his knee.

'Mummy!' he shouted again.

Abby looked at Braindead, who went to get up then abruptly sat down again. 'He wants you,' he said. 'His mum.'

'But I can't—' she began.

'You can,' said Braindead.

She looked back over at Logan then got out of her chair and ran to him shouting, 'I'm coming, Mummy's coming.'

*

'So tell me how on earth you escaped your hen party tonight?' Daniel asked Cassie.

Cassie shrugged. 'I gave them a telling-off about what they did to Ollie. I told them… well, I told them they were on their own. I was all done.'

'You told them off for me?' said Ollie.

'Yes,' she nodded. 'I'm having nothing to do with them for the rest of the trip.'

'Wow,' said Ollie. 'But what about your wedding? You'll have to see them then, won't you?'

Cassie stared at him for a long moment before she glanced at Katy.

'Let's just say I have a plan for that,' said Cassie.

Katy smiled back at her and nodded.

'Will you be okay?' asked Ollie.

Again she paused.

'I actually think I'm going to be,' she replied.

'I will propose a toast,' said Gabriel, suddenly standing up with Silvie in his arms.

'Oh yes, good idea,' said Katy.

'We have weathered some storms on this intrepid journey,' he said. 'But I think you will agree that we have all got to our intended destination.'

'Hear, hear,' said Braindead, taking Abby's hand.

'Hear, hear,' said Ollie, smiling at Cassie.

'Hear, hear,' said Daniel, gazing adoringly at his husband and daughter.

'So we shall raise a toast to weathering this storm together because when you are in a storm with the right people it's barely a storm at all.'

'I think he's already drunk,' admitted Daniel. 'Finish up now, love, before you ruin it.'

'To the best fellow travellers I could wish for,' Gabriel said, raising his glass high.

'Hear, hear,' they all agreed, standing up.

Ben reached for Katy's hand as they sat down and gave it a squeeze.

'Can I ask one tiny favour whilst we are all full of bonhomie?' he asked. 'Could Katy and I possibly have a head start on the way home, like maybe an hour? You know, it really is a pity to waste that honeymoon suite...'

Epilogue

Katy sat back at her desk the following Monday morning and wondered if she had ever been on holiday. Sure, the agency hadn't collapsed without her and the launch of Began vegan bacon seemed to have run smoothly, but a crisis with another client had erupted whilst she'd been away. Not one of her colleagues had arrived in her office that morning to ask if she had enjoyed her break but all of them trooped in one after another to give their version of the cock-up the previous week and why it wasn't their fault. She'd hoped that one of them would perhaps comment that she at least 'looked well' but no, none of them did. They were too busy covering their own backs.

She'd been sad to leave the hotel in the end. It had not been the holiday anyone was expecting but it had certainly had its moments. More chaos and drama than calm and relaxation.

They'd waved goodbye to Ollie the day after their wonderful meal at Francisco's and it was surprisingly emotional. Even though they'd only known him for less than a week, they had been through so much together that it felt much longer. Katy felt some kind of maternal instinct towards him which was weird and indeed he had thanked her for looking after him, which was even more weird. They'd all promised to keep in touch and Ollie had even said he would invite them all to his twenty-seventh birthday in Winchester in a couple of months.

He'd decided he needed a party since he'd missed out on a wedding that year. He also stated that it would be a grown-up party so would they mind leaving the children at home, at which they had all cheered whole-heartedly.

'A hotel room without children in it?' said Ben. 'Finally!'

Katy grinned at him. The honeymoon suite still hadn't been used for its intended purpose. They'd ended up staying at the restaurant until way after the kids' bedtime as everyone had been having such a good time and then nobody could be bothered to move beds again. They all slept in their bedrooms soundly with their children fast asleep beside them.

Ollie had also said that he would like to invite Cassie and her husband to his birthday party as long as she didn't bring any party games! He'd asked Katy to be sure to pass the message on to her.

Katy had spent two hours on the phone with Cassie the previous day when she had rung her in floods of tears to inform her she had done the deed. She'd called off her wedding. Katy had sat and listened patiently as Cassie snivelled it out of her system, whilst constantly murmuring that she knew it was the right thing to do and thanking Katy profusely for all her help. They'd ended the call eventually with Katy promising to check in with her today; she knew Cassie was nervous as it was her first day back at work.

'Hiya,' said Cassie when she picked up the phone.

'How are you doing?' asked Katy.

'Oh, not bad,' said Cassie. 'Fi's not talking to me. Jules's sister rang her last night and told her so at least I didn't have to announce it as Fi's already put something on Instagram. She says she's taking Jules out for a drink tonight to help drown his sorrows.'

'How kind of her,' said Katy sarcastically. 'Have you seen Ruth?'

'Funny you should ask that,' replied Cassie. 'She came to find me. I thought she was going to be mad because she'd put all that effort into my hen party but she came and apologised.'

'No way!' said Katy.

'Yeah, I know,' said Cassie. 'She said she could tell I wasn't happy and she was sorry she didn't say anything. She said she just got caught up in making sure it was a crazy hen party because that is what every bride-to-be wants.'

'Wow, I can't believe she said that,' replied Katy.

'She even said she wasn't going to organise any more hen parties. She said she's had enough. She wasn't enjoying it any more.'

'That is not what I was expecting you to say,' said Katy.

'And she said I'd done the right thing. She was proud of me and if I ever wanted to talk about it to give her a shout.'

'Well, that's brilliant,' said Katy. 'That must help make you feel a bit better.'

'It does,' agreed Cassie. 'I thought everyone would think I was awful but, well, people do actually seem to understand.'

'Because you're not awful and they know you would have done it for all the right reasons,' said Katy.

'Thank you.'

'Speaking of people who don't think you're awful, I forgot to tell you yesterday that Ollie made me promise to invite you to his birthday party that he's decided to have because he missed out on his wedding. He also invited your fiancé but of course he wasn't to know what was about to happen.'

'Oh,' said Cassie. 'How lovely. But perhaps he won't want me to come if he thinks I'm coming on my own?'

'Don't be stupid, of course he will. We're all going. I can't wait. He's said no kids so it's doubly exciting.'

'So Abby and Daniel and everyone?'

'Yes. You up for it? It's in Winchester so we could come and pick you up if you want, on the way.'

'Well, er…' stuttered Cassie.

'The best thing you can do when you find yourself single again is say yes to everything,' said Katy. 'So do you want to come?'

'Yes,' said Cassie. 'I do.'

'There you go,' laughed Katy. 'I guarantee you that will be the best "I do" you say all year.'

As she put the phone down it struck her that spending time with Ollie and Cassie had been a real bonus of their holiday. It had made them all realise how lucky they were to have found the one and to have wonderful kids in their lives, even if it didn't feel like that sometimes. The reality of the hen party had made Abby realise that too and the fact that it had forced her and Braindead to confront how unhappy she was had clearly had an impact. Braindead had already asked Ben if he would be interested in doing a babysitting swap on Friday nights. One Friday, Braindead would babysit Millie and Jack so Ben and Katy could go out, and the next Friday, Ben would look after Logan. Everyone seemed delighted with the idea, especially Abby, who had already planned where she and Braindead were going to go for the next six months.

It had been a good holiday, Katy thought. Utter chaos, but good. But then that's families for you.

Daniel appeared at the door of her office somehow looking a lot more tanned than she did.

'So, where are we going next year?' he asked.

She threw a pen at him.

A Letter from Tracy

Dear Reader

I want to say a huge thank you for choosing to read *No-one Ever Has Sex on Holiday*. If you enjoyed reading it and want to keep up to date with all my latest releases, just sign up at the following link. Your email address will never be shared and you can unsubscribe at any time.

www.bookouture.com/tracy-bloom

I really hope you enjoyed *No-one Ever Has Sex on Holiday* and if you did, I would be hugely grateful if you could write a review on your seller's website. I'd love to hear what you thought and it makes such a difference helping new readers to discover my books for the first time.

I would love to hear from you directly and you can get in touch on my Facebook page, via Twitter, Goodreads or my website.

Many thanks
Tracy

tracybloomwrites

7075043.Tracy_Bloom

@TracyBBloom

www.tracybloom.com

Acknowledgements

Thank you to Jenny Geras, my editor, who is so fond of the characters in these books that she came up with the idea of taking them on holiday! It's been a blast and I have thoroughly enjoyed reliving the trials and tribulations of the heady mixture of sand, sea, sun and small children.

As ever, thank you to the entire team at Bookouture who pull out all the stops to send a book on its way and also to Madeleine Milburn and her team at the agency who do such a great job behind the scenes.

I would also like to say thank you to you guys, my readers, who keep coming back for more. It is so much appreciated. And wherever you are, I sincerely hope you manage a lovely holiday this year. Enjoy!